Student Book

Fiona Beddall and Annette Flavel

Contents

UNIT 1
How do we find our way?

| Reading 1 | **Fiction:** Benny and Jenny Go to School | Page 8 |
| Reading 2 | **Factual text:** My Weekend in Sydney, Australia | Page 14 |

UNIT 2
How do we know about the past?

| Reading 1 | **Fiction:** Dinosaur World | Page 24 |
| Reading 2 | **Factual text:** Tutankhamun's Treasure | Page 30 |

UNIT 3
Why do we go on vacation?

| Reading 1 | **Fiction:** A Relaxing Vacation | Page 40 |
| Reading 2 | **Factual text:** Summer Camp Reviews | Page 46 |

UNIT 4
Why do we tell stories?

| Reading 1 | **Fiction:** Jane and the Sunflower | Page 56 |
| Reading 2 | **Factual text:** What are Myths and Legends? | Page 62 |

UNIT 5
Why take care of the environment?

| Reading 1 | **Fiction:** Meadow Rescue | Page 72 |
| Reading 2 | **Factual text:** Air Pollution. What Can you Do? | Page 78 |

UNIT 6
Why do we use numbers every day?

| Reading 1 | **Fiction:** A Gift for Grace | Page 88 |
| Reading 2 | **Factual text:** The Tick Tock of Time | Page 94 |

UNIT 7 — What do we do for entertainment?

Reading 1 — **Fiction:** An Entertaining Afternoon — Page 104

Reading 2 — **Factual text:** Youth Music News — Page 110

UNIT 8 — Why is space interesting?

Reading 1 — **Fiction:** Blue Jay and the Moon — Page 120

Reading 2 — **Factual text:** Life on the International Space Station — Page 126

UNIT 9 — How are homes different?

Reading 1 — **Fiction:** The Perfect Home — Page 136

Reading 2 — **Factual text:** Where We Live: Amsterdam — Page 142

UNIT 10 — How do we take care of our body?

Reading 1 — **Fiction:** Doctor Martina — Page 152

Reading 2 — **Factual text:** Say NO to Germs — Page 158

UNIT 11 — Why is Antarctica special?

Reading 1 — **Fiction:** An Extraordinary Expedition — Page 168

Reading 2 — **Factual text:** Adapting to Antarctica — Page 174

UNIT 12 — Why do we have festivals?

Reading 1 — **Fiction:** The Lantern Festival — Page 184

Reading 2 — **Factual text:** Spring Festivals Round the World — Page 190

How do we find our way?

Listening
- I can understand simple directions of how to walk somewhere.

Reading
- I can predict what a text is about from the title and pictures.

Speaking
- I can give simple directions using a map.

Writing
- I can write about a place I like.

1 💬 Look at the picture and discuss.

1 Who are these people?
2 Where are they?
3 What are they looking at?
4 What do they want to do?

2 💬 Discuss the places with a friend.

> movie theater   park
> playground   shopping mall
> grocery store   train station

1 How often do you go there?
2 Who goes with you?
3 How do you get there?
4 What do you do there?

3 ▶ 1-1 BBC Watch the video and match. What are the places on the map?

1 street   d
2 river   ☐
3 library   ☐
4 bank   ☐
5 restaurant   ☐
6 movie theater   ☐

5

Vocabulary 1

1 **Listen and repeat.**

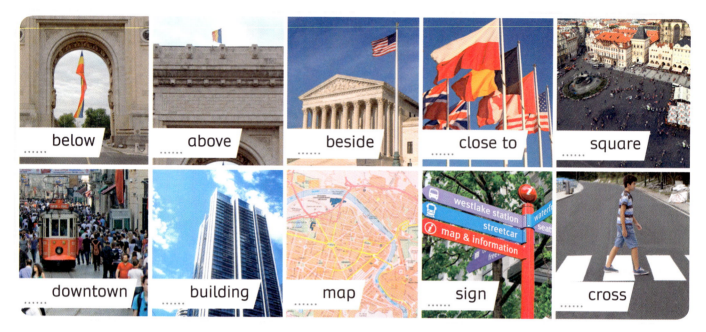

below | above | beside | close to | square
downtown | building | map | sign | cross

2 **Listen and number.**

3 **Look at the words in Activity 1 and sort.**

Places	Where things are	Things
	below	

4 **Read and circle.**

1. We live in the apartment (**above**) / **cross** Mrs. Garcia.
2. She's standing **close to** / **building** the sign.
3. I don't know where to go. I need to find a **sign** / **below**.
4. My favorite toy store is **building** / **downtown**.
5. The **building** / **beside** across from the bus station is a library.
6. There's a restaurant **beside** / **cross** her apartment.

5 Choose a city. Think of three buildings. Where are they?

The bus station in Milton City is beside the train station, on Franklin Square.

Pre-reading 1

1 **Look at the pictures, read the questions, and predict.**

1 Who are the important people and animals in the story? Are they good or bad?
2 Where are they?
3 What are they doing?
4 Why are they doing it?

2 Read the text and mark your predictions in Activity 1 correct (✓), incorrect (✗), or don't know (?).

Reading strategy
Use pictures to help you predict when you read a story. Ask *Who? Where? What? Why?*

A big man with two large bags is walking into the train station. The mice quickly run between his legs. Then Pedro hears the woman shout! He looks back. She's on the floor, and the big man is talking to her and trying to help her get up.

Reading 1

3 🎧 1.04 Read *Benny and Jenny Go to School*. Who is Jake? Where is he? What does he need for the school concert? Why?

> 📖 **Reading strategy**
>
> Use pictures to help you predict when you read a story.
> Ask *Who? Where? What? Why?*

Benny and Jenny Go to School

Benny and Jenny are cats. They live with Jake and his dad in an apartment in the city **above** a store. Jake is their best friend in the world!

It's time for school. Jake is taking his guitar to school today because he's playing in a concert. He's taking a giraffe toy in his backpack, too. He shows it to the cats. "This is my lucky giraffe," he says. "I never make mistakes in concerts when I have it with me. My grandma gave it to me when I was born".

Dad takes Jake to school. They walk to school today. Suddenly, Benny sees something on the table – Jake's giraffe! "Oh, no!" he says. "Jake needs that for his concert." "Let's take it to him at school," says Jenny.

lucky giraffe

Benny picks up the giraffe in his mouth and Jenny looks at a **map**. Then the two cats run out of the apartment and down the stairs very quickly. "First, turn left," Jenny tells Benny.

8

They turn left outside the **building** and soon they come to the train station **downtown**. They turn right. There's a big **square** in front of them. "Next, **cross** the **square**," says Jenny. "Jake's school is across from us!"

They run into the school. Jenny sees Jake's backpack on the desk. "Look!" she says. "Here it is. Let's put the giraffe in it." Benny jumps onto the chair **beside** the backpack and puts the giraffe inside.

concert

Later, Jake plays in the concert. He doesn't make any mistakes. Jake looks at his lucky giraffe and smiles to himself. Benny and Jenny smile, too!

4 Read the story again and circle.

1 Jake is a **boy** / **cat**.
2 The cats **like** / **don't like** Jake.
3 Jake needs his guitar for a **class** / **concert** at school.
4 Jake doesn't take his **giraffe** / **guitar** to school.
5 The cats **get a bus** / **run** to school.

5 Discuss with a friend.

1 How do animals in the real world find their way?
2 What do you sometimes forget to do? How can you help yourself to remember things?
3 Do you have a lucky toy or other lucky object? Describe it.

9

Grammar 1

1 Watch Part 1 of the story video and complete.

First, ... the road here and then .... right.

2 Read the grammar box and circle.

> **Grammar**
>
> | ✓ | ✗ |
> |---|---|
> | **Cross** the street here. | **Don't cross** the street here. |
> | Please **say** your name. | Please **don't say** your name. |
> | **Turn** left at the square. | **Don't turn** left at the square. |
>
> 1 The sentences above are **questions** / **instructions**.
> 2 People use *please* when they **want** / **don't want** to be polite.

3 Read *Benny and Jenny Go to School* again. Find and circle Jenny's instructions to Benny.

10

4 Match the sentences to the pictures. Then circle.

a

b

c

1 **Cross** / **Don't cross** the street now.
2 Please **ride** / **don't ride** your bike here.
3 **Brush** / **Don't brush** your teeth.
4 **Turn** / **Don't turn** left for the party.
5 Please **walk** / **don't walk** on the grass.
6 **Swim** / **Don't swim** in the ocean.

d

e

f

Listening and Speaking

> 💬 **Speaking strategy**
>
> Speak towards the listener.

5 🎧 1-05 Look at the map. Listen and find the way. Write letters from a to d in the correct boxes.

1 playground ☐
2 Lemon Tree Restaurant ☐
3 bookstore ☐
4 movie theater ☐

6 💬 Look at the map again. Then ask for directions from the shopping mall to these places.

bank   bus station   library   park

Excuse me. How can I get to the bus station from here?

First, turn left. Then look to your left. It's across from the Lemon Tree Restaurant.

11

Vocabulary 2

1 🎧 1-06 **Listen and repeat.**

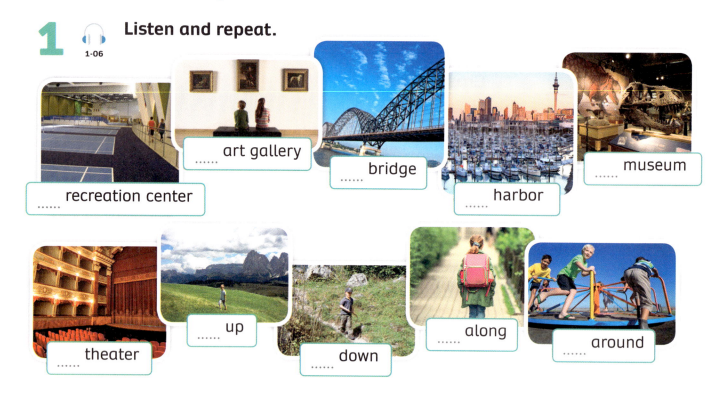

art gallery · bridge · museum · recreation center · harbor

theater · up · down · along · around

2 🎧 1-07 **Listen and number.**

3 Look at the map and complete the instructions for the race. Use words from Activity 1.

First run ¹ .... the lake. Then run ² .... the mountain and ³ .... it again. Next, run ⁴ .... the street to the finish.

12

4 Where should these people go? Write words from Activity 1.

1. I want to see old things.
   museum
2. We want to play badminton.
   ....
3. I want to look at the boats.
   ....
4. We want to look at pictures.
   ....

5 Imagine you can go to four of the places in Activity 1 this weekend. Write them in order, from your first choice to your last choice. Discuss your choices with a friend.

.... , ...
.... , ...

> I don't want to go to a recreation center because I don't like playing sports.

Pre-reading 2

Reading strategy
Use headings in a text to predict what it's about.

1 Look at the headings from a blog. Predict what the blog is about. Check (✓).

different kinds of vacation ☐   a vacation in a city ☐   a place in a city ☐

Friday: the Dubai Mall
Thursday morning: Dubai by boat
Saturday afternoon: Dubai Museum
Saturday morning: the Burj Khalifa

2 Read this paragraph from the same blog. Was your guess right?

FRIDAY: THE DUBAI MALL

I spent the Friday of my holiday at the Dubai Mall. There isn't anywhere like this at home! It has more than 1,200 shops, an ice rink, an aquarium, and some very big fountains.

Reading 2

3 🎧 1-08 Read *My Weekend in Sydney, Australia*. Look at the headings in the blog and predict what it is about.

Reading strategy

Use headings in a text to predict what it's about.

My Weekend in Sydney, Australia
by Mia Britt

Sydney Opera House

AN ART GALLERY AND OPERA HOUSE

On Saturday morning, we visited an **art gallery**. There were some beautiful paintings there. Then we walked **around** Sydney Opera House. It's an amazing building! Inside, there are four **theatres**. People perform in concerts there every evening.

After lunch, we climbed **up** onto Sydney Harbour **Bridge** and crossed the **harbour**. It was very noisy because they're repairing the bridge at the moment. However, it's an amazing walk with incredible views! When you look **down**, you can see the Opera House. After our walk, we went in the swimming pool below the bridge. It's the biggest swimming pool I've ever seen! It was lots of fun!

A WALK ON THE BRIDGE

1

DUGONGS AT THE AQUARIUM

On Sunday morning, we visited an aquarium because I'm learning about sealife at school this month. My favourite animals were the dugongs. People sometimes call them sea cows. They eat about 50kg of sea grass every day!

THE SHIP MUSEUM

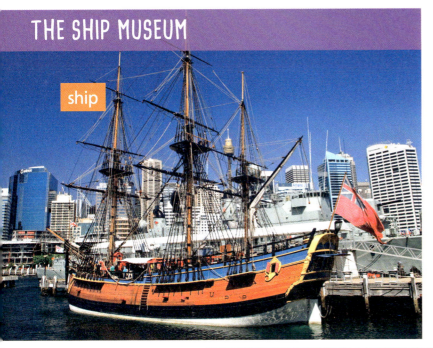

On Sunday afternoon we were at the Ship **Museum**. It's near the aquarium, and it's great! You can find out about Aboriginal boats. The Aborigines were the first people in Australia. You can walk around an old British ship, too. It was the first ship from Europe in this part of Australia. I really enjoyed walking around the ship!

4 Read the blog again. Circle **T** (true) or **F** (false).

1 Mia liked the art gallery.   T F
2 There aren't a lot of concerts at Sydney Opera House. T F
3 Mia was on a bridge above the harbor.   T F
4 Mia wasn't very happy at the swimming pool.   T F
5 Mia liked the dugongs.   T F
6 An Aborigine is a kind of boat.   T F

5 How do you think Mia found her way around Sydney?

15

Grammar 2

1   Watch Part 2 of the story video. Read and circle.

1. Kim and the Doctor are walking around **London** / **New York** today.
2. The Doctor **sometimes** / **never** travels in space and time in the TARDIS.
3. Kim is looking for a **good** / **bad** alien at the moment. Its name is the Smogator.

2 Look at the grammar box and read.

3 Read *My weekend in Sydney, Australia* again and complete.

1. People _____ in concerts there every evening.
2. They _____ the bridge at the moment.
3. I _____ about sealife at school this month.
4. People sometimes _____ them sea cows.

> **Grammar**
>
> Where **does** the Doctor **live**? He **lives** in the blue box.
>
> **Does** he **often come** to London? Yes, he **does**.
>
> He **doesn't visit** London **every day**.
>
> He and Kim **sometimes travel** in space and time.
>
> What **are** you **doing** here? **I'm walking** around the city.
>
> **Are** you **looking** for aliens **today**? Yes, I **am**.
>
> Kim **isn't running at the moment**. She**'s walking**.

4 Look and read. Then make two lists in your notebooks.

My routines
I go to Grandma's house every weekend.
I don't cycle to school every day.

Things I'm doing now
I'm sitting on a chair.
I'm not talking.

5 Look and read. Then ask and answer with a friend.

1 What language / you / speak ? (usually, at the moment)

> What language do you usually speak?

> What language are you speaking at the moment?

2 What / you / do ? (on Saturdays, now)
3 What book(s) / you / read ? (usually, this week)
4 Where / you / sit in class ? (every day, at the moment)

Speaking

6 How is today different from other Sundays? Look, point, and say.

> She's riding a scooter today, but she usually rides a bike.

Today

Other Sundays

7   Watch Part 3 of the story video. Where does Kim see the Smogator?

17

Writing

1 Look at the brochure quickly. Does it answer these questions?

1 What kind of place is it?
2 How do you get there?
3 What can you do there?

2 Read the brochure again and check your answers.

COME TO

RIPTON SPORTS CENTER

OPEN EVERY DAY OF THE WEEK!

You can do 32 different sports at this fantastic sports center!

Outside the building, you can play hockey, soccer, rugby, and tennis. Inside, there's a big room for gymnastics and an amazing swimming pool. There are rooms for judo, dance, and basketball, too.

Do you want to stay in shape and make new friends?

Then find out about our excellent classes. You can do them after school and on weekends. After your class, come to the restaurant for some food and drink with your friends.

And don't forget the store. It has lots of great sports clothes.

Where is it?

Trent Road, Ripton. From the train station, go along Long Road, and turn left opposite the theater.

JOIN A CLASS TODAY!

3 Read the brochure again. Find and circle the different words for *very good*.

4 **WB 15** Find or draw pictures of a recreation center. Then go to the Workbook to do the writing activity.

Writing strategy

Use different words for *very good*: *amazing, fantastic, great, awesome.*

18

Now I Know

1 How do we find our way?
Look back through Unit 1 and make a list.

We find our way using
....maps...... , ... , ... , ... , ...

2 Choose a project.

Make a presentation about your neighborhood or city.

1 Work with some friends.
2 Read your friends' brochures from Activity 4.
3 Together, choose your favorite places in your area.
4 Plan a presentation about them.
5 Give your presentation to the class.

or

Make a travel blog about a day in a city in another country.

1 Find out about places in the city.
2 Decide which places to visit.
3 Find or draw pictures of the places.
4 Write a travel blog about a day there.
5 Show your blog to the class.

Read and circle for yourself.

I can understand simple directions of how to walk somewhere.

I can give simple directions using a map.

I can predict what a text is about from the title and pictures.

I can write about a place I like.

2

How do we know about the past?

Listening
- I can understand the main information in simple dialogs.

Reading
- I can infer information in a text.

Speaking
- I can talk about jobs I know.

Writing
- I can write about an animal I like.

1 Look at the picture and discuss.

1 Where are the children?
2 What are they looking at?
3 Are the children interested in what they are doing?
4 Do you like this place?

2 Discuss with a friend.

1 Do you go to museums with your family or friends?
2 What kind of museum do you like to visit?
3 Do you have any museums in your neighborhood?
3 How can we learn about the past in a museum?

3 Watch the video. What is the name of the dinosaur? Then answer true (T) or false (F)

1 It didn't eat meat. ......
2 It had very big, sharp teeth. ......
3 The stegosaurus ate meat. ......
4 The stegosaurus had a small brain. ......

21

Vocabulary 1

1 🎧 1-09 **Listen and repeat.**

herbivore · carnivore · dinosaur · horn · tail
extinct · quick · careful · loud · dead

2 🎧 1-10 **Listen and number.**

3 **Read and match.**

1 You should be very careful when
2 Whales move their
3 You can only see dinosaurs
4 A lion is a
5 You can't see animals at the zoo

a carnivore.
b when you watch movies.
c when they're extinct.
d tails when they swim.
e you're close to a crocodile.

4 💬 **Describe an animal. Use words from Activity 1. Your friend guesses the animal.**

cheetah · donkey · frog · goat · rabbit · shark

> It's a herbivore. It has a short tail, but it doesn't have **horns**. It's **quick**, but it isn't **loud**. It can be brown, black, gray, or white.

> It's a rabbit!

22

Pre-reading 1

1 Look at the picture and guess the answers to the questions.

 Reading strategy
Use the time and place of a story to help you understand.

1 Where are the people and animals in the story?
2 Do the children live in the present, the future, or the past? And the animals?
3 What do you know about the time and place of the story? Compare your ideas with a friend.

2 Read the text. Are any of your ideas about time and place in the story?

A WORLD LONG AGO

Barl and Lom are fishing. Two little mammoths come to the river. "Look!" says Barl. "They want to be friends with us." "We can't be friends with mammoths," says Lom. "They're usually our dinner, not our friends!"

23

Reading 1

3 Read *Dinosaur World*. Why is Tilly amazed?

> **Reading strategy**
>
> Use the time and place of a story to help you understand.

DINOSAUR WORLD

"Can you take this picture to the cupboard, please, children?" asks Tilly and Sam's mum. They're helping her at the **Dinosaur** Museum where she works as a museum curator. The picture shows a green T-Rex. "Were all T-Rexes green?" asks Tilly.
"We know their shape because we find their bones under the ground. Paleontologists study dinosaurs and fossils," says Mum. "But we don't know their colour for sure."
The children **carefully** take the picture to the cupboard. It's very dark inside. They can't find a light and they can't find the back of the cupboard. "Something strange is going on!" thinks Tilly.

They quietly walk out of the cupboard into a forest.
They see a big animal with three **horns**.
"It's a triceratops," says Sam quietly.
Tilly is amazed. She thought dinosaurs were **extinct**!

24

Outside the forest, the children see a lake. A very big animal with a long **tail** is drinking there. "Wow! A diplodocus!" says Tilly. She really thought dinosaurs were **dead**. Another dinosaur is walking slowly to the water. "That's a stegosaurus! They're **herbivores**." says Sam.

Suddenly, they hear a **loud** roar and they see a T-Rex. "Oh, no!" screams Tilly loudly. "A **carnivore**!" Sam and Tilly run back into the forest quickly. The T-Rex runs after them. He's big but can run very fast! Sam sees the cupboard door between the trees. "This way!" he says. "Be **quick**! The T-Rex is running in our direction!"
They run to safety and they find the cupboard door. Back to the museum at last! What an adventure!

4 Read the story again. Circle T (true) or F (false).

1 Tilly and Sam's mother thinks all T-Rexes were green. T F
2 The children find a world with dinosaurs. T F
3 The first dinosaur they see is a triceratops. T F
4 A stegosaurus is drinking water from the lake. T F
5 Tilly and Sam run from the T-Rex because it's a herbivore. T F

5 Discuss with a friend.

1 Do Tilly and Sam make it back to the museum?
2 Why are museums important?

Grammar 1

1   Watch Parts 1 and 2 of the story video. What color are the dinosaur's eyes? Then read and write.

> carefully   quickly   quietly   slowly

Shh! It's a museum. There are rules. Talk 1 .... Walk 2 .... and 3 ....

Wow! Lots of rules! OK. Let's look for the Smogator 4 ....

2 Read the grammar box and complete the sentences.

Grammar

Be **quiet**.   Open the door **quietly**.
You're too **loud**.   You're speaking too **loudly**.
Kim is too **slow**.   Kim is walking too **slowly**.
Be **careful**.   Walk **carefully**.
We need to be **quick**.   We need to go **quickly**.
The dinosaur is **fast**.   The dinosaur can run **fast**.

1 The ___green___ words describe people and things.
2 The .... words describe actions.
3 To change a green word to a blue word, you can usually add ....
4 .... can be a green word or a blue word.

3 Read *Dinosaur World* again. Circle the blue words from the grammar box.

26

4 Read and circle.

1 Oh, no! There's a T-Rex behind us, and it's roaring **loud / loudly**. I think it's hungry!
2 Let's run! Be **quick / quickly**!
3 We're running too **slow / slowly**. The T-Rex is coming!
4 Let's think **fast / quick**. Where can we go?

5 Work in pairs. Choose a word or phrase from each box and do the action. Your friend guesses and says what it is.

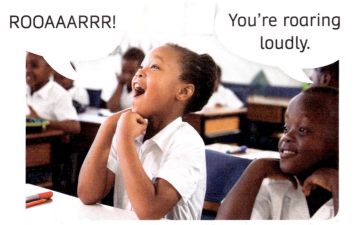

ROOAAARRR!

You're roaring loudly.

| carefully | fast | loudly |
| quietly | sadly | slowly |

close a door
pick up a dinosaur egg
roar   run   walk

Listening

6 Listen and write 1, 2, or 3.
1-12

Look carefully. ☐   Walk quickly. ☐   Walk slowly. ☐
Study quietly. ☐   Walk carefully. 1   Don't talk loudly. ☐

7 Listen again. Match the places from A–C to the dialogs from 1–3.
1-13

A street in a town or city ☐
B library ☐
C outdoor swimming pool ☐

27

Vocabulary 2

1 **Listen and repeat.**

pharaoh   bury   archeologist   treasure   thieves

dig   exhibit   gold   steps   1 tomb

2 **Listen and number.**

3 **Read and write words from Activity 1.**

1 These are words for people. ....
2 People often walk up and down these. ....
3 Thieves like to take these things. ....
4 You can do these activities in sand. ....
5 We put people here when they die. ....
6 You can see this in a museum. ....

4 **Work with a friend. Choose a word from Activity 1. Make words using as many letters as possible.**

great   *eat*   *ear*   *tear*   *gate*

28

5 💬 Discuss with a friend.

1. Are there a lot of old things in your neighborhood? What kind of things are they?
2. Think of your favorite museum. What exhibits do you like there?
3. Why do archeologists dig in the ground?
4. "One man's trash is another man's treasure." What treasure do you have? Do your friends agree that it's treasure?

Pre-reading 2

1 💡 Read the first sentence of each paragraph in a magazine article. Choose the best title for the article.

> **Reading strategy**
>
> Read the first sentence of each paragraph to get the general idea of a text.

- Pompeii, in the past and today ☐
- The buildings and people of Pompeii ☐
- Life in the busy city of Pompeii ☐

1. 2,000 years ago, Pompeii was a busy city.
2. Everything changed suddenly one day about 1,950 years ago.
3. For more than 1,700 years, the buildings were under the ground.
4. Now, more than two million people visit Pompeii every year.

2 💡 Look quickly at the text on the next page. Read the first sentence of each paragraph. Choose the best title for the article.

- A pharaoh's life ☐
- Treasure in the tomb ☐
- Egypt's great past ☐

29

Reading 2

3 🎧 1-16 Read *Tutankhamun's Treasure*. Check your answer from Activity 2.

Reading strategy

Read the first sentence of each paragraph to get the general idea of a text.

TUTANKHAMUN'S Treasure

3,300 years ago, a boy named Tutankhamun was **Pharaoh** of Egypt. He died when he was 18. His body was **buried** in a **tomb**. With him, they buried chairs, lamps, beds, clothes, games, small boats, food and drink, and boxes of **treasure**. They thought that he needed them in his next life.

An **archeologist** named Howard Carter looked for Tutankhamun's tomb for many years. In 1922, he said to his men, "We have to stop. I don't have any more money."

Four days later, one of his men shouted, "There's a **step** in the sand." All the men started to **dig**.

The next day, there were 12 steps, and below them, a door. Carter looked inside. There was a lot of gold! All the things for Tutankhamun's next life were there. And inside a gold box, there was an amazing **gold** mask and the body of the pharaoh.

Today, the things from the tomb are usually an **exhibit** in a museum in Cairo. But they often travel to different museums around the world.

Tutankhamun's mask

30

There were tombs for other pharaohs, too. **Thieves** discovered them, and soon there was no treasure in the tombs. But thieves didn't find Tutankhamun's treasure.

Did you know?

We call this picture writing *hieroglyphs*. The writing on the tomb walls tells the story of the **pharaoh's** life.

4 Read the article again. Answer the questions.

1. How old was Tutankhamun when he died?
2. Why did his people put a lot of things in his tomb?
3. Why was there no treasure in the tombs of the other pharaohs?
4. What does the writing on the tomb walls describe?
5. In 1922, Carter didn't have much time to look for Tutankhamun's tomb. Why?
6. Where in his tomb was Tutankhamun's body?
7. In which city can people usually see Tutankhamun's treasure?

5 Think about things that are important in your life. Make a list, then compare with a friend.

Grammar 2

1   Watch Part 3 of the story video. Where are they? Then read and write.

We have to .... the Smogator.

2 Look at the grammar box and read.

Grammar

You **have to** listen carefully.

Do I **have to** walk slowly? No, you **don't**.

The Doctor **has to** push the buttons carefully.

Does Kim **have to** help? No, she **doesn't**. The Doctor can do it.

You **don't have to** talk quietly.

3 Read *Tutankhamun's Treasure* again. Find and circle a sentence with *have to*.

4 Read the old letter and complete it with the phrases.

Dear Father,   Egypt, 1923

I have a new job! I'm working for Howard Carter at the tomb of Tutankhamun. I ¹ [e] pictures of all the things in the tomb. Carter ² [ ] about everything, and the other men ³ [ ] the things carefully out of the tomb.
We are all living close to the tomb. Everyone is super friendly, and we have a chef, so we ⁴ [ ]. There are a lot of dangerous snakes in the sand, but Mother ⁵ [ ] about me. I'm always very careful.
With all my love,
Harry

---

a have to move   **c** doesn't have to worry   **e** ~~have to take~~

b has to write   **d** don't have to cook

5 Sue is an archeologist. She's talking to Will about her job. Listen and circle the things she has to do.

work at night   talk on the phone
work on a computer   examine old things
work outside all the time
work on the weekend

6 Write about Sue with *have to* and *don't have to*. Use the information in Activity 5 and your own ideas.

They have to examine very old things.

....

....

....

....

Speaking

7 Work with a friend. Choose a job. Then ask and guess.

> ** Speaking strategy**
>
> Focus on the speaker.

chef   cleaner   dentist   doctor   hairdresser
mechanic   pilot   police officer   teacher   vet

You: Do you have to work outside?
Friend: No, I don't. I have to work inside.
You: When do you have to work?
Friend: In the day, and at night, and on weekends, too.
You: Do you have to help sick people?
Friend: Yes, I do.
You: You're a doctor!

33

Writing

1 Look at the picture of a horned tortoise. Describe it and answer. Then guess the answers to the questions.

1. Where does it live?
2. Is it alive today, or is it extinct?
3. Is it a herbivore or a carnivore?
4. Is it fast or slow?
5. Is it dangerous? Why? / Why not?

2 Read a webpage from *The Time Traveler's Nature Guide* and check your answers.

Horned tortoise

DO YOU WANT TO SEE A HORNED TORTOISE? THEN YOU HAVE TO TRAVEL TO AUSTRALIA, AND GO BACK IN TIME ABOUT 2,000 YEARS.

This animal is much bigger than a modern tortoise. It has a shell, horns on its head, and a long tail. It has strong legs , and it's good at digging. It eats plants, not people, and it moves very slowly. But you have to be careful around it because it can hurt you with its tail.

DON'T GET TOO CLOSE!

3 Read the webpage again. Find and circle useful words and phrases to describe an extinct animal.

4 Find or draw a picture of an animal you like. Then go to the Workbook to do the writing activity.

✏️ Writing strategy

Use interesting words and phrases to describe an animal.
This animal is much bigger than a modern tortoise.

34

Now I know

1 How do we know about the past?
Look back through Unit 2 and make a list.

We learn about the past thanks to
.....exhibits..... ....

2 Choose a project.

Perform a scene from a movie about time travelers and extinct animals.

1 Work with some friends.
2 Decide what extinct animal(s) the time travelers see in the scene.
3 Write some words for the scene.
4 Practice and then perform the scene to the class.

or

Make an interesting webpage for your museum.

1 Work with some friends. Choose a subject for your museum (e.g. science).
2 Choose a name for it.
3 Think of some interesting exhibits. Find or draw pictures and make labels.
4 Write a webpage for it.

Read and circle for yourself.

I can understand the main information in simple dialogs.

I can infer information in a text.

I can talk about jobs I know.

I can write about an animal I like.

35

3

Why do we go on vacation?

Listening
- I can understand activities that happened in the past.

Reading
- I can identify the structure of a story.

Speaking
- I can talk about an event in the past.

Writing
- I can write about a vacation in the past.

1 💬 **Look at the picture and discuss.**

1 What can you see in the picture?
2 What are they doing?
3 Do you sometimes do this?

2 💬 **Think and check (✓). Discuss with a friend.**

1 What is your favorite place to go on vacation?

the beach ☐ the mountains ☐

2 How do you get there?

by bus ☐ by plane ☐
by boat ☐ by car ☐

3 Who do you go on vacation with?

parents ☐ grandparents ☐
cousins ☐ friends ☐

3 ▶ 3-1 BBC **Watch the video. What are the two teams building?**

🇬🇧 British	🇺🇸 American
bonnet	hood

37

Vocabulary 1

1 🎧 1-18 Listen and repeat.

 campsite
 blanket
 sleeping bag
 camping stove
 flashlight

 compass
 set up a tent
 make a fire
 clean up
 get lost

2 🎧 1-19 Listen and number.

3 Read and write a word from Activity 1.

1. You put it on your legs when you are cold or sit on it at a picnic.
2. You do this so you can sleep in it.
3. It happens when you don't know where you are going.
4. You cook on it outside. It uses gas.
5. You put things in their place and you take away dirty things.

4 Look and write words from Activity 1.

1 2 3 4 5

38

5 Look at Activity 1. Think and group the things you take camping. Write them in the chart.

things that go inside a tent   both   things that go outside a tent

6 Think and write more things you can take when you go camping.

Pre-reading 1

> **Reading strategy**
>
> Find the beginning, middle, and end of a story to help you follow the action.

1 Read and match.

1 beginning ☐
2 middle ☐
3 end ☐

a   My sister and I made a big sandcastle. Then we dug a hole and covered Grandpa. We put a big sun hat on his head.

b   We stayed at the beach all day and went home at sunset. It was a great day.

c   Yesterday was the first day of vacation. I woke up and packed my bag for a day at the beach.

2 Read and circle.

1   The **beginning** / **end** finishes the story.
2   The **beginning** / **end** of a story tells us about the place and characters.
3   The **end** / **middle** is where the story develops.

39

Reading 1

3 🎧 1-20 Read *A Relaxing Vacation*. Was the vacation relaxing for Ben's dad? Why? / Why not?

📖 **Reading strategy**

Find the beginning, middle, and end of a story to help you follow the action.

A Relaxing Vacation

Last weekend, Ben and his family went camping. They arrived at the **campsite** on Saturday. "It's real quiet here! It's perfect for a relaxing vacation," said Dad.

On Saturday afternoon, they **set up the tent**. Mom put the **blankets** and **sleeping bags** inside. In the evening, they **made a fire**. Ben and his sister, Bess, played with the **flashlight** in the tent. Mom made everyone hot chocolates to stay warm. Ben told a scary story about a bear and Bess checked for bear prints around the tent.

The next morning was sunny. Dad cooked eggs on the **camping stove**, for breakfast. Ben and Bess helped wash the dishes.

I love being outdoors. Let's go hiking!

It's my first hike!

After a while Bess stopped suddenly. "Look! Bear prints." she whispered quietly. She was scared!

40

They walked along the path some more.
They looked at the map and the **compass**.
It didn't help. "We **got lost**," said Bess.
They saw a big, dark, brown shape.
"Stop! Wait!" said a voice. It was a hiker
with a furry hat and a brown
jacket. It wasn't a bear!

It's getting dark.
Where is the campsite?

hiker

What's that?
Is it a bear?

Later they all **cleaned** up the campsite and
they drove home. The children slept in the car.

They arrived home very late that night. Mom closed
the door and said, "Well, that was a fun vacation."
Dad didn't say anything. He just
made a face. Maybe camping
wasn't for them after all!

5 Read and write *B* (beginning),
M (middle), or *E* (end).

1 They arrived home. ....

2 They drove to the campsite. ....

3 The hiker helped them. ....

4 Read the story again and circle.

1 Ben and Bess went **camping** /
to an amusement park.

2 They **got** / **didn't get** lost.

3 Ben and Bess **walked** / **swam**
along the path.

4 The vacation **was** / **wasn't**
relaxing for Ben's dad.

6 Discuss with a friend.

1 Was your last vacation
relaxing? Which parts were
not relaxing?

2 Did you get lost?

3 Did you see any animals?

41

Grammar 1

1   Watch Parts 1 and 2 of the story video. What does the old man do? Then read and write.

swam   made   took   put   sang

We ¹ _____ the tents off the bikes and we ² _____ the blankets on the ground. Next we ³ _____ a fire, we ⁴ _____ a song, and we ⁵ _____ in the river.

2 Read the grammar box and write A, B or C.

Grammar

a   The children **explored**. Dad **wanted** a relaxing vacation.

b   I **made** a fire. We **went** to the beach last vacation. The children **slept** all the way home.

c   The map **didn't help**. They **didn't know** the way.

1   Verbs in the past end in **-ed**.

2   To say what you did not do in the past use **didn't** + verb.

3   Some verbs in the past don't end in **-ed**.

3 Read *A Relaxing Vacation* again and circle the verbs in the past.

4 Read and match.

1. I swam in the river.
2. She made a fire.
3. We drove to the campsite.
4. He explored.
5. I climbed a tree.

a. She didn't make a fire.
b. You/They didn't swim in the river.
c. We didn't drive to the campsite.
d. I didn't climb a tree.
e. He didn't explore.

Listening and Speaking 1

Speaking strategy
Speak clearly.

5 Listen and take notes about the vacations. What didn't Alicia do?

	Abby	Alicia	Colin
Place	beach		
People	family		
Transportation	car		
Activities	walked at the beach, swam, ate ice cream		

6 Tell a friend about your last vacation.

What did you do on your last vacation?

I went camping by the river but we didn't swim in the river. It was too cold!

43

Vocabulary 2

1 🎧 1-22 Listen and repeat.

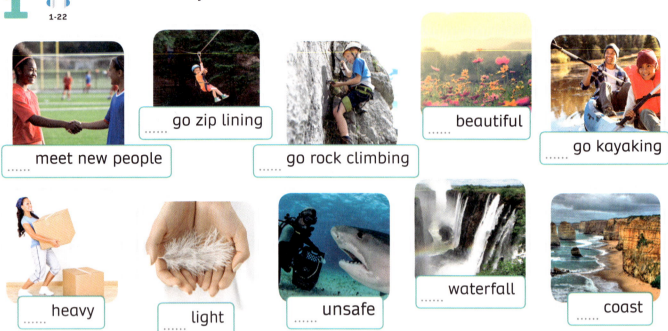

meet new people · go zip lining · go rock climbing · beautiful · go kayaking
heavy · light · unsafe · waterfall · coast

2 Look at the words in Activity 1. Underline the describing words. Check (✓) the places. Circle the outdoor activities.

3 💡 Write the outdoor activities from Activity 1 on the line.

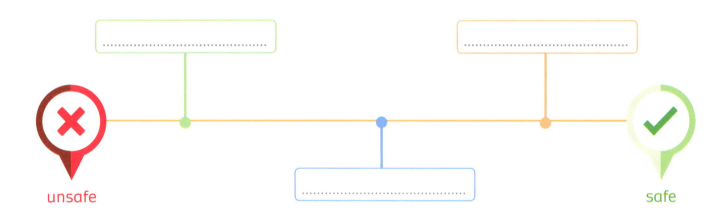

unsafe — safe

4 🎧 1-23 Listen and write the word.

1. coast
2. ....
3. ....
4. ....
5. ....
6. ....

44

5 Read and match. Then ask a friend.

1 Do you like meeting
2 Where can you go rock
3 Do you think going zip
4 Do you live close to
5 Do you like safe or

a lining is unsafe?
b the coast?
c climbing in your country?
d unsafe activities?
e people?

Pre-reading 2

1 Read the review. Did Lisa like the rock climbing center?

> **Reading strategy**
> Decide which part of a text to read again to find information.

The RADICAL ROCK Climbing Centre

This school was amazing. I took a four-week course. I didn't know how to climb before, but I do now! I wanted to learn to climb to be ready for my summer rock climbing camp. I went in the afternoons after school and on Saturday mornings.
They gave us special shoes and a helmet because it's important to be safe.

Lisa, aged 10

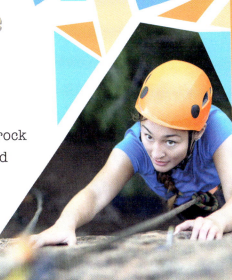

2 Read the review again and answer the questions.

1 Did Lisa write a good or bad review?
2 Did Lisa know how to climb before?
3 Why did she take the course?
4 Why did they give her special shoes and a helmet?

Reading 2

3 Read *Summer Camp Reviews*. Which camp was bad?

> 📖 **Reading strategy**
>
> Decide which part of a text to read again to find information.

SUMMER CAMP Reviews

Did you go to summer camp last year?
Where did you go?
What did you do?
Who did you meet?
Did you have fun?

TELL US ALL ABOUT IT …!

life jacket

1

I went to sports camp on the **coast**. I loved it! We **went rock climbing** and **zip lining**. We swam and we **went kayaking** near a **waterfall**. It wasn't **unsafe** because we had life jackets.

★★★★★

Paul Smith

scenery

2

We went to performing arts camp. We learned a play and we made all the scenery. It was **beautiful**! Then our parents came to watch the play. Performing in front of all those people was scary but it was lots of fun. ★★★★

Leo and Sandy Black

certificate

TECHNOLOGY CAMP
completed by Ben Jones
15 August, 2018

3

I really enjoyed technology camp last month. **I met lots of great people**. They all loved computers and science, just like me! I learned new things and I even made a computer game. The tutors were friendly and the food was good.

⭐⭐⭐⭐⭐

Mario Tuccio

...tutor

4

I went to Maths camp last summer but I didn't do any Maths at all! I painted a house and tidied up a garden. The weather was terrible and the tutors were mean. I **met new people** but they were miserable too. ⭐

Susie Wallace

4 Read the text again and number in order.

technology ☐
sports ☐ 1
maths ☐
performing arts ☐

5 💬 Answer the questions with a friend.

1 Did Paul go to sports camp?
2 Did Paul play volleyball?
3 Did Leo and Sandy learn a play?
4 Did Mario like technology camp?
5 Did Marta meet new people?

6 Answer the questions.

1 What was the problem at math camp?
....
2 Who did Sandy go to camp with?
....
3 Where was the sports camp?
....
4 When was technology camp?
....
5 How many sports did Paul do?
....

7 💡 Which kind of camp do you like? Why do children go to summer camp?

47

Grammar 2

1   Watch Part 3 of the story video. What did Kim use to take the trash out of the water?

Did you throw all this rubbish on the ground?

2 Read the grammar box and complete.

Grammar

a **Did** Marta **go** to summer camp?   Yes, she **did**.
   Did you **like** the tutors?   No, I **didn't**.
   _____ they learn to **make** scenery?   Yes, _____.

b **What did** you **do** at camp?   I **made** a video game.
   Where did she **go**?   She **went** to the coast.
   Why did Paul **go** to sports camp?   He **went** there because he likes sports.
   Who did they **meet**?   They **met** new people.
   How did you **get** there?   We **went** by car.
   When _____ Mario **make** a computer game?   He _____ a computer game last month.

48

3 Read *Summer Camp Reviews* again. Find and underline questions with *Wh-* words and circle the time phrases.

> We can use time phrases to talk about the past.
>
> yesterday
> the day before yesterday
> last week
> last summer/month/year/night

4 Read and circle.

1 Did they go rock climbing?
   a Yes, they did.   b Yes, I did.
2 What did you play?
   a He played baseball.   b We played volleyball.
3 Where did you go last summer?
   a I went on vacation to the mountains.   b I went with my family.
4 Did she go hiking last month?
   a No, he didn't.   b Yes, she did.

Listening and Speaking 2

5 🎧 1-25 Listen and write the names.

~~Rita~~   Brendon   David   Susan

Find someone who …

| went to the beach last summer. | went horseback riding last year. Rita |
| enjoyed school last week. | played sports yesterday. |

6 Ask your friends. Use the ideas in Activity 3 and change the time phrases if you can.

Did you stay home last vacation?

No, I didn't.

Where did you go?

Last year, I went to the mountains.

49

Writing

1 Read Mina's postcard. What did she like about the vacation?

2 Read Mina's postcard again and answer the questions.

1. Where did Mina go?
2. Who did she go with?
3. Did she enjoy visiting the museums?
4. What amazing thing did she see at the reserve?
5. Did she go rock climbing?
6. Why was it a great vacation?

A Great Vacation

Last winter, I went to Michoacán in Mexico with my mom and dad. We went by bus. We slept on the bus because it was a long way.

On the first day, we visited museums. I didn't like the museums, but my parents loved them.

The next day we took a taxi to the Monarch Butterfly Biosphere Reserve. We saw millions of beautiful butterflies. It was amazing!

On the last day, we walked in the forest. We ate lunch beside a waterfall. Then we went zip lining. I loved it!

It was a great vacation. I saw new things and I was with my family.

3 Read the postcard again. Find and circle the time phrases.

4 Find or draw pictures of a vacation. Then go to the Workbook to do the writing activity.

> **Writing strategy**
>
> Use time phrases *last winter*, *on the first day*, *the next day* to write about the past. They help to structure your writing.

Now I Know

1 Why do we go on vacation? Look back through Unit 3 and make a list.

We go on vacation to meet people.

2 Choose a project.

Do a class survey about vacations last year.

1. Work in groups. Think of five questions to ask about vacations.
2. Do a survey. Ask people your questions. Record their answers.
3. Make a bar graph to present your results.
4. Present the results of the survey to the class.

or

Invent your own summer camp.

1. Choose a summer camp you would like (e.g. sports camp, science camp).
2. Find or draw pictures of the place and the activities, and write some notes.
3. Make a poster about your camp.
4. Show your poster to the class.

Read and circle for yourself.

I can understand activities that happened in the past.

I can identify the structure of a story.

I can talk about an event in the past.

I can write about a vacation in the past.

4

Why do we tell stories

Listening
- I can follow the sequence of events in a simple story.

Reading
- I can understand the correct sequence of events in a simple story.

Speaking
- I can ask for information about an event.

Writing
- I can write a simple story.

1 💬 Look at the picture and discuss.

1 Who can you see?
2 Where are they?
3 What are they doing? Why?
4 Do you think the children are enjoying themselves? Why / Why not?

2 💬 Discuss with a friend.

1 When do you tell stories?
2 Who tells good stories in your family?
3 Do you prefer reading by yourself or listening to a story? Why?
4 What's your favorite story? Why do you like it?

3 ▶ 4-1 BBC Watch the video and answer the questions.

1 What's the name of the festival the presenter is attending?
2 How much does a medieval suit of armor weigh?

53

Vocabulary 1

1 **Listen and repeat.**

giant | castle | bowl | coin | silver
enormous | furious | prince | princess | fairy tale

2 **Read and write a word from Activity 1.**

1 A very big building with strong walls.
2 Someone in a story who is very, very big.
3 A story for children.
4 A male member of a royal family.
5 An adjective that means very, very big.
6 A coin can be made of gold or ... .

3 **Read and circle.**

1 The **furious** / **prince** lived in the palace.
2 I eat my cereal from a **castle** / **bowl**.
3 Sofia loved **fairy tales** / **enormous**.
4 My mom was very, very mad. She was **furious** / **enormous**.
5 A giant lives in a **castle** / **bowl**.
6 Is that a **bowl** / **silver** coin?

54

4 💬 Discuss with a friend. ❓

1. Do you like reading fairy tales?
2. Can you think of a story with a giant in it?
3. How often do you read books?
4. Is there a castle in your country?

Pre-reading 1

1 Read the story. Do you know it in your language?

> **Reading strategy**
> Recall the order of events to help you understand a story.

Once upon a time there was a boy called Jack. One day his mother said, "Jack, we have no food. We have to sell the cow. Can you take her to market?"

On the way to town Jack met a man. The man said, "I want to buy your cow. Can I give you these super beans?" So, Jack gave him the cow and took the beans home. His mother was very angry because he didn't go to the market. She threw the beans into the yard.

2 💡 Read the story again. Number the sentences in order.

..... Jack's mother threw the beans away.

..... Jack met a man.

..1.. Jack's mother asked, "Can you take the cow to market?"

..... Jack went home.

..... The man gave Jack some magic beans for the cow.

..... Jack's mother was furious.

55

Reading 1

3 Read *Jane and the Sunflower*. Why was the giant angry?

> 📖 **Reading strategy**
>
> Recall the order of events to help you understand a story.

Jane and the Sunflower

Once upon a time there was a girl called Jane. She loved reading **fairy tales** and she loved doing math.

One day, Jane's mother asked her to buy bread. Jane went to the store and bought a small sunflower, but no bread. When she came home her mother was **furious**. She threw the plant out the window.

The next morning Jane woke up and saw that the sunflower was **enormous**. She climbed right to the top.

There she found a **castle**. Inside the castle was a long table with three **silver bowls**. And sitting at the table was a **giant**.

"I can solve puzzles very well. I'm the champion at math," said the giant. He was cross and wanted to see if the little girl was good at math.

"OK, but if I solve them, you give me the bowls." said Jane.

56

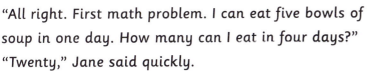

"All right. First math problem. I can eat five bowls of soup in one day. How many can I eat in four days?"
"Twenty," Jane said quickly.
"Oh, boo!" said the giant. The answer was right. "One more problem. If you are wrong, I keep the bowls!" said the giant, showing his yellow teeth. "I have thirty silver **coins** and someone takes fifteen. How many do I have?"

Jane took a deep breath. "Um … fifteen." Jane won the bowls. But the giant was angry and he ran after Jane. Jane ran away and climbed down the sunflower. Then she cut down the plant and it seemed like the giant was trapped at the top. But then Jane realized that the giant was just lonely. She invited him to dinner and he jumped onto a pile of pillows and went home with Jane. Jane gave the bowls to her mother and they all lived happily ever after.

4 Read and match. Then number in order.

..... Jane climbed up   the sunflower to a giant's castle.
..... Her mother was   the sunflower and cut it down.
..... The giant was   a sunflower plant at the store.
..... Jane climbed down   angry and threw the plant away.
  1   Jane bought   cross with Jane.

5 Fairy tales often have a problem and a solution. What was the problem and what was the solution in this tale?

Grammar 1

1 Watch Part 1 of the story video. Why did they have a party? Then read and circle the verbs.

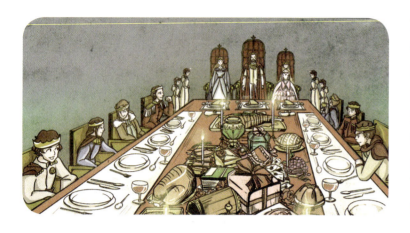

In the kitchen, they made the food and put gold bowls on the long table. Many princes came from near and far. They wore beautiful clothes, said wonderful things to the princess, gave her presents and ate delicious food. That night the princess met a wonderful man.

2 Read the grammar box and complete. Then match the words.

Grammar

present		past
come	–	came
take	–	....
put	–	....
get	–	....
meet	–	....

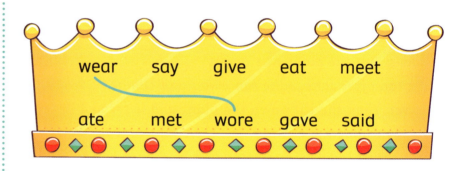

3 Read *Jane and the Sunflower* again. Find and circle the verbs in the past that don't end in *-ed*. Then complete the chart.

is/are	was/were	run away	ran away
buy		see	
come	came	take	took
cut down		throw	
find		wake up	
go	went	win	

58

4 Ask and answer the questions with a friend. Use complete sentences.

1 Where did Jane go?
2 What did she buy?
3 What did Jane's mother do with it?
4 What did Jane find at the top of the sunflower?
5 What did Jane win from the giant?
6 What did she do to the sunflower in the end?
7 What did Jane do with the silver bowls?

> She went to the store.

Listening and Speaking 1

5 🎧 1-28 Listen and check (✓) the fairy tale.

Little Red Riding Hood ☐   The Ugly Duckling ☐

The Three Billy Goats Gruff ☐

6 🎧 1-29 Listen again and number in order.

Me? But I'm an ugly duckling. ☐

The spring came. The ugly duckling left the barn and went back to the pond. He was very thirsty and put his beak into the water. He saw a beautiful, white bird! [1]

It's you! ☐

Wow! Who's that? ☐

Not any more. You're a beautiful swan, like me. Do you want to be my friend? ☐

All the other animals watched as the two swans flew away, friends forever. ☐

Yes! ☐

7  Discuss with a friend.

1 Was the ugly duckling really a duck? What was he?
2 What does the story teach us?
3 Do you have a best friend?
4 Do you like acting?
5 Is it possible to tell stories without words?

59

Vocabulary 2

1 Listen and repeat.

king queen fierce wife hero
husband myth legend search hide

2 Listen and number.

3 Read and write a word from Activity 1.

1 Children do this when they play.
2 These are words for people.
3 A person who is admired for their bravery.
4 Two kinds of stories.

4 Think and match.

1 king   a wife
2 husband   b myth
3 hide   c queen
4 prince   d search
5 legend   e princess

5 In Activity 4 the pairs are often key in stories. Can you think of any other characters you might see in stories?

60

Pre-reading 2

1 Read the project. What's the child's favorite legend?

> **Reading strategy**
> Use visual representations to help you understand.

The Legend of Robin Hood

In the past, there weren't any books. People told stories about famous men and women. They told the stories many times and the details changed over time. The stories became legends.

My favorite legend is Robin Hood. It's about a man who lived in Sherwood Forest around 600 years ago. People were sad because the scary Sheriff of Nottingham took all their gold.

Robin Hood and his friends, the Merry Men, were very good at using bows and arrows. They lived in the woods. They took gold from those who had too much and gave it to people who had nothing.

2 Think and complete the mind map.

| lived 600 years ago | Sheriff of Nottingham | Sherwood Forest |

- gave gold to people who had nothing
- took gold from people who had too much

plot — place — characters

Merry Men

61

Reading 2

3 Read *What are Myths and Legends?* What is a myth?

 Reading strategy

Use visual representations to help you understand.

What are Myths and Legends?

Stories have been important since the beginning of civilisation. Myths and legends are types of story that are part of people's culture and tradition. Old people often tell them to young people, so they can live on for a long time.

What is a myth?

A **myth** is a story with a purpose. Ancient civilisations used **myths** to explain natural events like storms, floods, strong winds and seasons. The plot often has a **hero searching** for something on a long and dangerous journey.

In ancient times, people believed that gods and goddesses controlled nature on Earth. Many myths feature gods. Who are Greek gods? They include: Zeus, god of the sky and thunder, Poseidon, god of the sea, earthquakes and horses, and Athena, goddess of wisdom and war. Look at this map to show the different ancient cultures who used myths as stories.

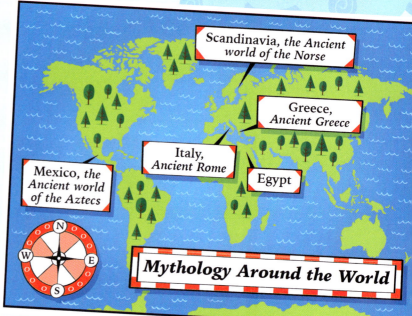

Mythology Around the World

What is a legend?

A **legend** is a story about people. It could be true and some parts of the story could come from real history. A legend usually has a **hero** as the main character. The hero isn't superhuman like the gods and goddesses in a myth, but is a man or woman who has extraordinary qualities. Legends are usually about a **fierce** fight between good and bad characters, and the hero wins.

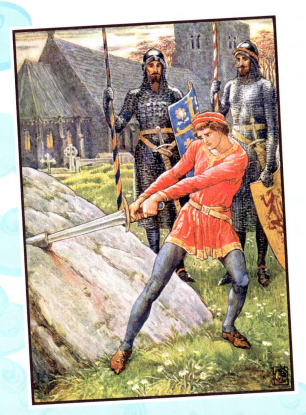

What are famous legends?

Let's look at two different legends. According to Celtic legend, **King** Arthur was the King of Camelot because he pulled a sword from a famous stone. We don't know if King Arthur and his **wife**, Queen Guinevere really lived. Above the Polish town of Zakopane, a mountain peak forms the outline of a sleeping man. The Sleeping Knight, the legend goes, will wake from his sleep if trouble comes, and rise to save Zakopane.

4 Discuss with a friend.

1. What kinds of stories are myths and legends?
2. What are the common features for a myth and a legend? Write a list.
3. Do people write these stories?
4. Who was King Arthur?
5. Who or what is the sleeping knight of Zakopane?
6. Do you know any other stories about the world around us?

Grammar 2

1 Watch Parts 2 and 3 of the story video. Then read and write.

What _____ it want?

Who _____ that?
What _____ that?

2 Read the grammar box and say.

> **Grammar**
>
> Who **was** that?
> What **was** that?
> Who **were** they?
> Where **were** the people?
>
> What **did** you **do**?
> Where **did** she **go**?
> When **did** she **arrive**?
> Who **did** he **ask**?
>
> **What happened**?
> **Who believed** in gods and goddesses?
> **Who had** a myth about a sleeping giant?

3 Read *What are Myths and Legends?* again. Circle the question words in the titles.

4 Match the questions and answers.

1 Who was the sleeping knight?
2 Who were the Merry Men?
3 What did you do yesterday?
4 Where did Robin Hood live?
5 Who became a swan?
6 What did people in Ancient Greece believe?

a I read three books.
b a mountain in Zakopane.
c He lived in the woods.
d They were Robin Hood's friends.
e The ugly duckling did.
f They believed that gods controlled nature on Earth.

5 Work in pairs. Ask each other the questions from Activity 4. Close your book when answering.

Who were the Merry Men? What happened in the Ugly Duckling?

Listening and Speaking 2

> **Speaking strategy**
> Face the speaker.

6 Read and answer the quiz.

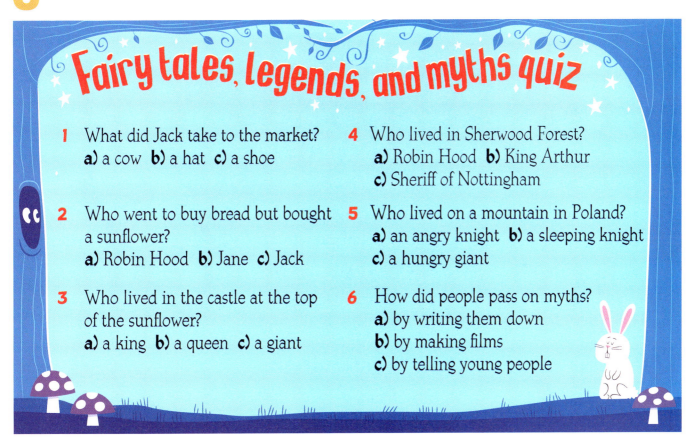

Fairy tales, legends, and myths quiz

1 What did Jack take to the market?
a) a cow b) a hat c) a shoe

2 Who went to buy bread but bought a sunflower?
a) Robin Hood b) Jane c) Jack

3 Who lived in the castle at the top of the sunflower?
a) a king b) a queen c) a giant

4 Who lived in Sherwood Forest?
a) Robin Hood b) King Arthur c) Sheriff of Nottingham

5 Who lived on a mountain in Poland?
a) an angry knight b) a sleeping knight c) a hungry giant

6 How did people pass on myths?
a) by writing them down
b) by making films
c) by telling young people

7 🎧 1-33 Listen and check your answers.

8 Write a quiz about fairy tales, legends, and myths. Ask your friends.

Who went … ?   Who ate … ?   Who made … ?   Who wanted … ?   What happened after … ?

What did (name) do … ?   What did (name) wear … ?   Why did he/she … ?   Where did … ?

What was the … ?   Who was/were … ?   Why was/were … ?

Writing

1 Read Luke's homework. What's the title of Luke's homework?

2 Read Luke's homework again and answer.

1. What characters does he like?
2. What does Luke think about scary characters?
3. Why does he like the Scary Queen?
4. How does the Scary Queen trick Snow White?

My Favorite Character

My favorite people in stories are the scary characters. I think they're interesting and funny.

I really like the Scary Queen from Snow White. She wanted to poison Snow White because she was kind. The Scary Queen wore a witch costume to find Snow White. She gave her a bad apple and Snow White slept. I liked the Scary Queen because she had powers and she was smart.

I like scary characters because they are important to a good story. Without the scary characters, there is nothing for the good characters to do. And anyway, there are scary people in the real world, too.

3 Read Luke's homework again. Underline the reasons Luke gives for his choices.

4 Find or draw a picture of your favorite character. Then go to the Workbook to do the writing activity.

Writing strategy

Give simple reasons for your opinions to make your writing stronger.
I think they're interesting and funny.
I like the Scary Queen because …

66

Now I Know

1 Why do we tell stories? Look back through Unit 4 and make a list.

We tell stories because we want to …

explain the world around us

2 Choose a project.

Write and perform a dialog.

1. Work in groups.
2. Think of scenes from stories you like. Decide on the characters and what they say.
3. Write the dialog in your notebook. Practice the dialog.
4. Perform the dialog for the class.

or

Research a myth and make a poster.

1. Work in pairs.
2. Choose a myth you know.
3. Make a poster with images, key words, and a title.
4. Show your poster to the class.

Read and circle for yourself.

I can follow the sequence of events in a simple story.

I can ask for information about an event.

I can understand the correct sequence of events in a simple story.

I can write a simple story.

Why take care of the environment?

Listening
- I can identify the context in which an everyday conversation is taking place.

Reading
- I can predict what a text is about from the title and pictures.

Speaking
- I can compare different kinds of transportation.

Writing
- I can write a short text about the environment.

1 💬 Look at the picture and discuss.

1 What can you see in the picture?
2 Where do the things in the picture come from?
3 What happens to places like this after many years?

2 💬 Discuss with a friend.

1 The average American family produces over 728 kg of waste a year. Do you think this is a problem? Why? / Why not?
2 What can we do if we want less trash?

3 ▶ 5-1 BBC Watch the video. What problems does it talk about? Check (✓).

air pollution ☐   noise pollution ☐
water pollution ☐   litter ☐

4 💡 Which kinds of pollution are a problem in your city or neighborhood?

69

Vocabulary 1

1 🎧 **Listen and repeat.**
1-34

country | fresh air | plant | insect | habitat
wildlife | pretty | full | rescue | throw away

2 🎧 **Listen and number.**
1-35

3 **Read and match.**

1 Your backyard can be a great habitat for
2 There's litter on the ground because the trash can is
3 A lot of wildlife lives at the
4 I like walking in the country to get some
5 The flowers on those plants are very
6 Remember to throw away

a park.
b fresh air.
c insects.
d your trash.
e pretty.
f full.

4 💬 **Discuss with a friend. What habitats can you think of? Add words to the mind map.**

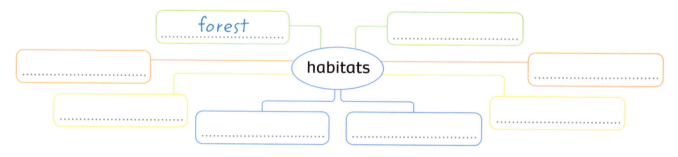

forest — habitats

70

5 When did you last go for a walk in the country? Which habitat(s) were you in? What things from Activity 1 did you see?

Pre-reading 1

Reading strategy
Make predictions before you read and while you're reading.

1 Look at the picture and guess. Why are there a lot of balloons?

2 Read the start of the story. Why do the balloons have the number 200 on them? Guess the answer. Then continue reading and check your answer.

Balloons

"Three … two … one … go!" said the man, and hundreds of balloons flew up from the park into the air above. The balloons all had the number 200 on them because today the town is 200 years old.

Abbie and Josh looked at the balloons happily.
"They look pretty," said Abbie. "But where are they going?"
"To Britain," said Josh, "or to China! Sometimes balloons fly a very long way."

71

Reading 1

3 🎧 1-36 Read Part 1 of *Meadow Rescue*. Make predictions as you did for Activities 1 and 2.

> **Reading strategy**
> Make predictions before you read and while you're reading.

4 🎧 1-37 Read the rest of the story. When you think of a question, stop reading, and guess the answer. Then continue reading and check your answer.

Meadow Rescue

1 "Close your eyes," said the park ranger, Miss Tucker. The children were in a meadow in the **country**, on a science trip. "What can you hear?" The children listened. Then they described the noises of all the **insects** and birds around them.
"A meadow is a nicer **habitat** for **wildlife** than other fields," said Miss Tucker, "because it has long grass and a lot of flowers."

💡 **1** What do the children hear?

💡 **2** Does Miss Tucker say yes? Why? / Why not?

2 "Can we have our lunch now?" asked Juan. "I'm hungry."
"Sorry, you can't eat here. We don't want to leave any trash. It's dangerous for wildlife." Miss Tucker said.
Juan and Ava walked around the meadow together. Juan wasn't happy. "It's good to be outside in the **fresh air**. But the rules here are worse than the rules at school!" he said. "I often see trash in the country. What's the problem?"

72

3 The meadow was **full** of insects. "Those blue butterflies are my favorites," said Ava.
"I like the red and black ones," said Juan. "They're bigger than the blue ones, and they're **prettier**, too."

4 "What's in there?" asked Ava. They looked under a **plant** and saw a bottle. At the end of the bottle was a small, gray body with a long, thin tail. "It's a mouse!" said Juan. "It can't get its head out of the bottle!"
They called Miss Tucker. "Mice love to drink from bottles, but then they can't move. Many of them die."
Miss Tucker **rescued** the mouse.

5 Later, the children had lunch in the picnic area. "**Throw away** all your trash," said Juan. "Animals can die when we leave trash on the ground."

5 Read the story again and circle T (true) or F (false).

1 Meadows are usually dangerous places for animals.   T   F
2 The children had lunch in the meadow.   T   F
3 All of the mouse's body was in the bottle.   T   F
4 Miss Tucker helped the mouse.   T   F

6 Discuss with a friend.

1 The bottle in the story was dangerous for the mouse. What other litter can be dangerous for wildlife. Why?
2 When a trash can is full, what should you do with your litter?

73

Grammar 1

1   Watch Parts 1 and 2 of the story video. Why do the insects have green eyes? Then read and write.

"We are too slow. Slower than the Smogator."

"We need to be quicker."

"Oh, no! It's big and it's angry. It's .... us!"

2 Read the grammar box and complete the chart.

quick	*quicker*
slow	
big	
happy	
safe	

Grammar

It's **safer** in the TARDIS.

The Doctor was **happier** before the plant caught him.

We need to be **quicker**.

We were **slower than** the Smogator.

The Smogator is **bigger than** us.

3 Read *Meadow Rescue* again and complete.

"A meadow is a .... habitat for wildlife than other fields," said Miss Tucker.

"They're .... the blue ones and they're .... , too."

74

4 Think and compare the pictures. Use the words in the box or your own ideas.

| busy | clean | cloudy | cold | dirty |
| pretty | quiet | snowy | warm |

In the mountains it is snowier than in the field.

a

b

It's a **good** habitat for wildlife. It's **better** than other kinds of field.

The rules here are really **bad**. They're **worse** than the rules at school!

What **a lot** of insects! There are many **more** here than in the school.

Listening and Speaking

Speaking strategy
Offer suggestions.

5 Listen and number the pictures.
1-38

a

b

c

6 Imagine there's a lot of litter at your neighborhood park. What can you do to change this? Discuss with a friend and make suggestions.

Let's …

Why don't we …?

I think we should …

Great idea!

That's not a bad idea.

75

Vocabulary 2

1 Listen and repeat.
1-39

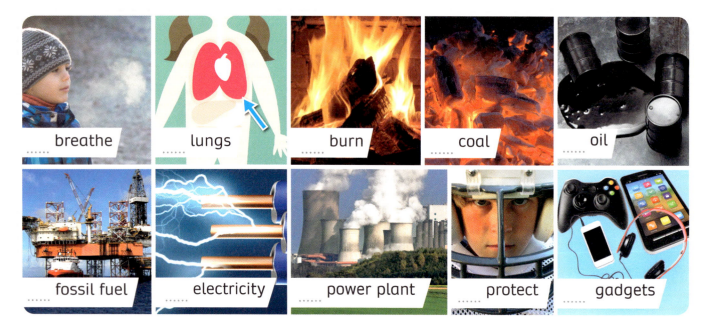

breathe | lungs | burn | coal | oil
fossil fuel | electricity | power plant | protect | gadgets

2 Listen and number.
1-40

3 Read and cross out the wrong word or phrase.

1 Please protect
   **the environment / me /
   your head / breathe**.

2 It smells in here because
   I burned some **food /
   paper / water / cardboard**.

3 Coal is **a fossil fuel / oil /
   black / from under the
   ground**.

4 We need electricity for **fridges
   / gadgets / lungs / lights**.

5 People often use fossil fuels
   when they **drink / drive cars /
   light fires / cook**.

4 Can you solve the code? Write a word from Activity 1 for each symbol.

Most people love ♥ like TVs, tablets, and game consoles. ♥ need ♦, or they stop working.

A lot of our ♦ come from big buidlings called ♠. The ♠ burn ♯ like coal and oil.

Pollution from the ♠ goes into the air. People ↻ the air, and the pollution goes go into their ✚.

1 ♥ ...gadgets...   4 ♯ ....
2 ♦ ....   5 ↻ ....
3 ♠ ....   6 ✚ ....

76

5 Discuss with a friend.

1. When do we breathe quickly? When do we breathe slowly? Why?
2. Are there any factories or power plants close to your home? Do you like living close to them? Why? / Why not?
3. Which gadgets do you and your family use every day?
4. Imagine there's no electricity for a week. You can't use any gadgets. How do you feel? Why?

Pre-reading 2

1 Read the text and underline anything that you don't understand.

> **Reading strategy**
>
> When you don't understand part of a text, read it again. Read the parts before and after it, too.

The world's forests are very important. Trees make oxygen, and without oxygen we can't breathe. So why do we cut down an area of forest bigger than twenty football pitches every minute? We should protect our trees, not cut them down.

2 Read the underlined parts of the text again, and the parts before and after them. Write *yes* or *no*.

1. Oxygen is important when we breathe. ....
2. The world's forests are bigger now than before. ....

Reading 2

3 Read *Air Pollution. What Can You Do?* What are the three main things you can do to help reduce air pollution?

> **Reading strategy**
>
> When you don't understand part of a text, read it again. Read the parts before and after it, too.

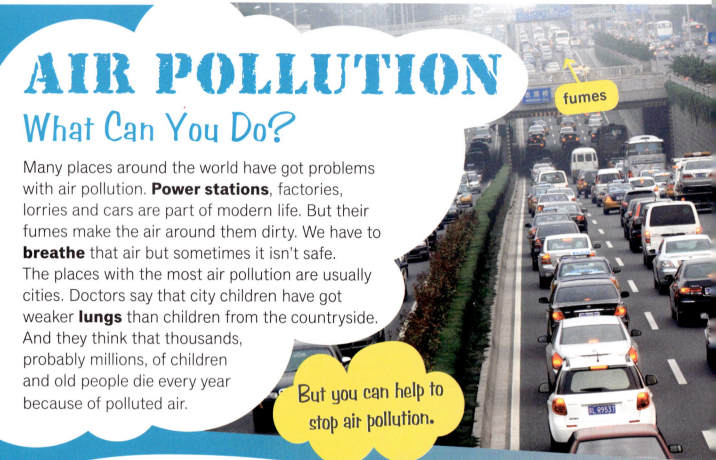

fumes

AIR POLLUTION
What Can You Do?

Many places around the world have got problems with air pollution. **Power stations**, factories, lorries and cars are part of modern life. But their fumes make the air around them dirty. We have to **breathe** that air but sometimes it isn't safe. The places with the most air pollution are usually cities. Doctors say that city children have got weaker **lungs** than children from the countryside. And they think that thousands, probably millions, of children and old people die every year because of polluted air.

But you can help to stop air pollution.

Here are some ideas:

 Walk or cycle to school

Lots of people think that driving is the safest way to get to school but they're wrong. Did you know air pollution is worse inside a car than outside on the street? Fumes from cars are one of the biggest causes of air pollution, too. Buses and trains are better than cars but the best way to travel is on foot or by bike. Choose the quietest streets, without much traffic. Cycling and walking keep you fit. They wake up your brain in the morning too, so you can get better grades at school!

2 Switch off your gadgets

When you are not using computers, TVs and other **gadgets**, switch them off. And switch off the light when you leave a room too. This saves **electricity**, and power stations don't have to **burn** so much **fossil fuel**.

switch off

3 Plant trees

Trees take some of the pollution out of the air. Can you plant a tree in your garden, your closest park or at school?

plant a tree

Together, let's protect our lungs and make our air fresh!

4 Answer the questions.

1 What health problem do some children in cities have?
2 Does more air pollution go into the lungs of people in cars or people walking and cycling?
3 What can help you to get better grades at school?
4 What can we do to save electricity?

5 Discuss with a friend.

1 How do you usually get to school? Do you like traveling this way?
2 Are you sometimes in places with air pollution? Where? How do you feel when you are there?
3 What do you do to stop air pollution?

79

Grammar 2

1   **Watch Part 3 of the story video and complete.**

The TARDIS is the _____ time machine on Earth, but it sometimes takes us to the _____ places.

2 Look at the grammar box and read.

Grammar

These bees are **the biggest** and **ugliest** on Earth.

Air pollution is one of **the worst** problems for the environment.

The best cars for the environment are electric cars.

Which country cuts down **the most** trees?

3 Read *Air Pollution. What Can You Do?* again and circle all the adjectives ending in *-est*. Then complete the chart.

quiet	quieter	the quietest
big		
safe	safer	the safest
ugly		
bad		
good		
many/a lot of		

80

4 Look and write sentences to compare the pictures.

big   fast   slow

Motorcycles are faster than bikes.
....
....

motorcycle

quad bike

bike

Speaking

5 You want to visit a friend in a different city. Look at the information. Then discuss.

Let's travel by train. It's the best for the environment.

Yes, but it's the slowest. I think we should go by plane. It's quicker.

Why don't we … ?

	🚆	✈️	🚗
people	156	88	4
time	4 hours	1 hour	3 hours
pollution (per person)	5 kg	100 kg	15 kg

6 Think about a trip that you often make. How do you travel? Is there a better way to go?

Writing

1 Look at the leaflet quickly. What habitat is it about?

2 Read the leaflet and answer the questions. In what order did you find the answers?
1 What problems are there in the habitat?
2 What should we do?
3 Why is this habitat important?

Protect Our Oceans

Our oceans are the biggest habitat on Earth, and home to many important marine species. Trash, overfishing, and chemicals that end up in our oceans mean we are destroying natural resources.

We should protect our oceans for future generations. We need to keep the oceans clean and not throw our trash on beaches. Plastic that ends up in the ocean is a real problem for marine animals and wildlife, destroying their habitats.

We need to reduce waste, save water and keep our oceans clear of trash. That's how we can protect our beautiful marine life for years to come.

We have to **stop** the pollution, take care of our fish, and protect our oceans!

3 Look at the leaflet again. Number the paragraphs with the (1) examples of the topic, (2) the information, and (3) the conclusion.

4 Find or draw a picture for your leaflet. Then go to the Workbook to do the writing activity.

Writing strategy

Use a structure when you write. Introduce the topic, give more information and then write a conclusion.
We need to reduce waste.

82

Now I Know

1 Why take care of the environment? Look back through Unit 5 and write sentences with the words in the box.

electricity   litter   poster   protect   travel   trees

We can tidy up our litter.

2 Choose a project.

Give a presentation about protecting habitats on Earth.

1. Work with some friends.
2. Read your friends' leaflets from Writing Activity 4.
3. Together, choose a habitat.
4. Plan a presentation about the best ways to protect it.
5. Present it to the class.

or

Write an article about a problem with the environment.

1. Find out about problems with the environment and ways that people are solving them.
2. Find or draw pictures and the ways to solve a problem.
3. Write a short article about it.
4. Show your article to the class.

Read and circle for yourself.

I can identify the context in which an everyday conversation is taking place.

I can compare different kinds of transportation.

I can predict what a text is about from the title and pictures.

I can write a short text about the environment.

83

6

Why do we use numbers every day?

Listening
- I can identify times and prices in short dialogs.

Reading
- I can extract factual details from a text.

Speaking
- I can ask questions about daily routines.

Writing
- I can write about a typical day at school using time words.

1 💬 **Look at the picture and discuss.**

1 What are the children doing?
2 What numbers can you see? Why are the numbers there?
3 What other sports do you know about? Are numbers important in these sports? How?
4 What other activities use numbers? How?

2 **Read and match the activities to the numbers.**

1 traveling by train, bus, or plane
2 reading a book
3 shopping
4 playing music
5 cooking

a 100 g
b
c $2.95
d Chapter 12
e 12:55

3 ▶ 6-1 BBC **Watch the video. Answer the questions.**

1 What time is it?
2 What do the children make with Nina?

85

Vocabulary 1

1 Listen and repeat.

go shopping | gift | stall | money | expensive
cheap | useful | colorful | choose | pay

2 Listen and number.

3 Look at the words in Activity 1 and sort.

Things	Actions	Descriptions
gift		

4 Complete the sentences with your own ideas.

1 When I go to a café, I sometimes choose _____.
2 My parents have to pay for my _____.
3 When I go shopping, I often buy _____.
4 My favorite colorful things are _____.
5 Some useful things in my classroom are _____.
6 At markets, I sometimes see stalls with a lot of _____.

86

5 Think of a gift that someone gave you. Ask and answer the questions with a friend. Can your friend guess what the gift is?

1 Who gave the gift to you? When?
2 Was it cheap or expensive?
3 What does it look like? Is it colorful?
4 Is it useful? What do you use it for?

Pre-reading 1

1 Look at the picture, read the questions, and guess. Then read the start of the story below to check.

> **Reading strategy**
>
> Compare the lives of the people in a story with your own.

1 How often do the family go shopping?
2 Where do they buy food?
3 How do they get there?
4 Who in the family likes going shopping? Who doesn't?
5 What do they like to buy?

"Why do we have to go shopping every Saturday?" said Ethan. "Grocery stores are boring." But Ethan's mom didn't listen. "Come on!" she said with a smile. "Let's get in the car."

"Can we buy ice cream?" asked Saskia, Ethan's little sister. She loved going to the grocery store and choosing her favorite food.

"Yes, we can. And Ethan can choose a pack of cookies, too."

2 Compare the family in the story with your family. What's the same? What's different?

Reading 1

3 Read *A Gift for Grace*. What are the children doing?

Reading strategy

Compare the lives of the people in a story with your own.

"What about that pair of earrings?" asked Jasmine. "Good idea! I really like them!" said her cousin, Alex. Alex was **shopping** for a birthday **gift** for his sister, Grace. Grace was turning 11!

Can I help you?

How much are those earrings, please?

They're twenty-two dollars.

Alex sighed. They were too **expensive**! He had saved and saved for his sister's birthday. They looked at the prices at a stationery stall. Jasmine loved stationery, but Alex wasn't so sure. Stationery didn't seem very interesting to him. There must be something he could buy for his big sister.

That pack of pens is **cheap**, and pens are always **useful**.

A pack of pens? That's a really boring gift! I know! I can buy her a bag of candy.

4 Read the story again and circle **T** (true) or **F** (false).

1 Jasmine is Alex's sister.   T F
2 Alex can pay for the earrings.   T F
3 Jasmine likes stationery, but Alex doesn't.   T F
4 Jasmine hates cheese.   T F
5 Alex paid five dollars for Grace's gift.   T F
6 Alex gave Grace some soap.   T F

Jasmine spent three dollars on a piece of cheese, but they didn't find a gift for Grace. They didn't see a candy stall, but they saw a **stall** with a lot of **colorful** soap. Alex **chose** a big bar of yellow soap. It smelled of lemons.
"It looks the same as my cheese!" laughed Jasmine.
"How much is it, please?" asked Alex.
"It's eight fifty for a big bar," the stallholder answered.
"Great!" he said. "I'd like a big bar, please. My sister loves soap."
Alex **paid** the stallholder. The cousins went home to prepare for the birthday celebrations.

Guess what happens next. Does Grace like her gift?

Later, Alex gave Grace her gift. She happily smelled the gift, and suddenly her face changed. Something was wrong!

Happy Birthday! This soap smells awesome. I hope you like it.

Thanks!

Very funny, Alex! This isn't soap. It's cheese!

 Discuss with a friend.

1 Who do you give gifts to? What gifts do you usually give?
2 Did you ever take something of someone else's by mistake? What was it? What happened?

Grammar 1

1 Watch Part 1 of the story video. Why does Kim buy things at the market? Then read and complete.

I bought a _____ of this, a _____ of that and a _____ of these.

2 Read the grammar box and match.

Grammar

1 Can we please open that **box of** cookies? c
2 I'd like **a** new **pair of** sandals.
3 Can I have **a piece of** cake?
4 I want to buy that **pack of** pencils.
5 There's a **bag of** grapes in the fridge.
6 I ate **a bar of** chocolate.

3 Read *A Gift for Grace* again. Find and match.

1 a bag of   a soap
2 a bar of   b earrings
3 a pack of   c pens
4 a pair of   d candy
5 a piece of   e cheese

90

4 Choose how many dollars you have (between five, six, nine, or ten). What can you buy? Look and say.

I have six dollars. I can buy a pair of shorts and a piece of pineapple.

Listening and Speaking 1

Speaking strategy
Have a complete conversation.

5 🎧 1-45 Listen and write the prices. What does Charlie buy?

store clerk

Charlie

1 board game ....
2 robot ....
3 action figure ....

6 Do a shopping role play. Use phrases from Activities 2 and 3 to help you.

Student A
1 Imagine you're a store clerk.
2 Find or draw things that people can buy in a grocery store.
3 Write the prices.
4 Help shoppers when they come in.
5 Then swap roles.

Student B
1 Imagine you're in a grocery store.
2 You have $25. Think about what you want to buy.
3 Go shopping.
4 Ask the store clerk about prices.
5 Then swap roles.

Vocabulary 2

1 **Listen and repeat.**

quarter · half · hour · minute · second · century · decade · shadow · invent · tell the time

It's eight o'clock.

2 **Listen and number.**

3 **Number from 1 (the shortest) to 8 (the longest).**

month ☐   decade ☐   second [1]   hour ☐
day ☐   year ☐   century ☐   minute ☐

4 **Complete the sentences with words from Activity 1.**

1 Ten years is a _____ .

2 When four people share something, each person should have a _____ .

3 On a sunny day, a tree makes a dark _____ on the ground.

4 Twelve hours is _____ a day.

5 When you _____ something, you make or think of it for the first time.

6 A _____ is ten decades.

92

5 Ask and answer these questions. Then think of more questions.

1 Where were you:
   a four hours ago?   b 30 minutes ago?   c ten seconds ago?
2 How long does it usually take you to:
   a get to school?   b brush your teeth?   c do your homework?

Pre-reading 2

Reading strategy

Use diagrams to help you understand a text.

1 Look at the diagrams and read. Which diagram shows the information best? Can you imagine this diagram as a video? What's happening?

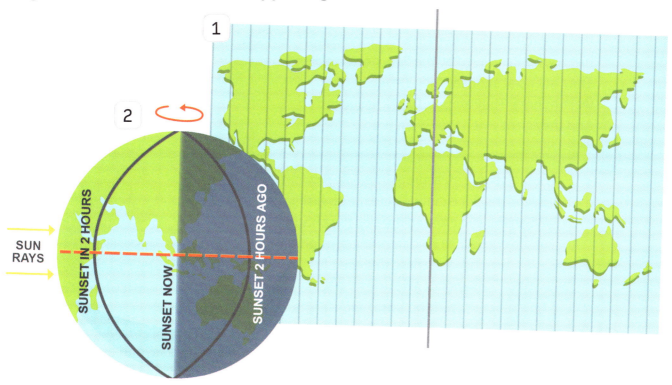

The Earth is constantly spinning around, but it completes one rotation around its axis about every 24 hours. The Sun is always in the sky above half of the Earth, but in the other half of the Earth, it's night.

Reading 2

2 🎧 1-48 Read *The Tick Tock of Time*. Match the pictures and diagrams from A to E to the paragraphs from 2 to 5.

> 📖 **Reading strategy**
> Use diagrams to help you understand a text.

The TICK TOCK of Time

A obelisk

01 Imagine a world without time. Without **quarter** to eight, or **half** past three, or midday, or midnight. It isn't easy because time is an important part of modern life. But for most of history, humans lived by the Sun, not a clock. They got up at sunrise. They ate when they were hungry. They stopped work at sunset. And they slept when they were tired.

02 Some people measured time. The Ancient Egyptians, for example, had tall obelisks. When the sun crossed the sky, the **shadow** of the obelisk fell on different marks on the ground, and these told the time. Sundials also used a shadow to **tell the time**, and were popular in many places.

03 Of course, sundials and obelisks didn't work on cloudy days or at night. In Ancient China, Greece and Rome, there were water clocks, too. Water ran slowly out of one bowl into another, and the water level told the time. ☐

D hands clock face pendulum

E digital clock battery

94

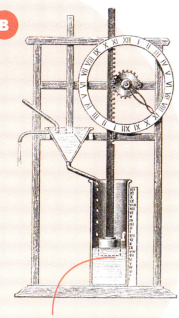

sundial

B Three and a half **centuries** ago in Holland, a man named Christiaan Huygens **invented** the first clock with a pendulum. When the pendulum moved from side to side with its tick tock sound, it moved the cogs inside the clock. The cogs moved the hands on the clock face. In the next **decades** and centuries, there were more and more clocks.

water level

05 Lots of modern clocks and watches are digital. They've got a battery and a very small quartz crystal inside. The numbers on the screen tell the time. Today there are clocks in every home and every classroom. We measure every day of our lives by **hours**, **minutes** and **seconds**.

04

3 Read the article again. Answer the questions.

1. When did most people get up in the past?
2. When did most people sleep in the past?
3. Can you tell the time with an obelisk on a cloudy day?
4. In what way were sundials the same as obelisks?
5. What makes the tick tock sound in a clock?
6. What kind of clocks have a screen?

4 Discuss with a friend.

1. What kind of clocks do you have at home? Do they have a pendulum? Do they have hands? Are they digital?
2. How often do you check the time on a school day / on Sundays / on vacation?
3. Imagine all the clocks in your home and school stop working suddenly. Is your life better or worse than before? Why?

95

Grammar 2

1   Watch Parts 2 and 3 of the story video. What do the Doctor and Kim do?

Kim and the Doctor traveled back in time: three o'clock, quarter till three, two thirty …

3 Read the first paragraph of *The Tick Tock of Time* again. Find these times and draw the minute hand.

2 Read the grammar box and put the times in order.

Grammar

What's the time?

It's eight o'clock.   It's eight thirty.

It's quarter after eight.   It's quarter till nine.

six thirty ☐

quarter till six 1

quarter after six ☐

six o'clock ☐

4 What do you do at these times? Look and say.

I get up at quarter after seven.

96

5 Look and match. Then tell the time.

1 2 3 4 5 6

a 07:00   b 02:30   c 07:45   d 03:15   e 12:15   f 04:45

08:00 eight   08:30 eight thirty
08:15 eight fifteen 08:45 eight forty-five

Listening and Speaking 2

6 1-49 Listen and number in order.

| have breakfast ☐ | take a bath ☐ | finish school ☐ |
| wake up [1] | do my homework ☐ | have lunch ☐ |

Arjun

7 1-50 Listen again and complete the clocks.

8 Work with a friend. Ask and answer about your routines on a school day.

What time do you get up?

At quarter after seven.

97

Writing

1 💬 Imagine you need to choose a new school. Which of these questions should a school website answer? Discuss your answers.

1 What time does the school day start and finish?
2 What subjects do the children learn?
3 When do they have recess and lunch?
4 Do the children enjoy school?

2 Read the website and find answers to the questions in Activity 1.

About us   Departments   Students   Parents   Contact us

A typical day at Hapgood Elementary School
by Tilly Gomez

The school day starts at eight o'clock. We do two hours of English in the morning, and other subjects like P.E., science, art, and music. Art is my favorite!

We have recess at eleven o'clock, and after that we eat our lunch. I usually have a pack of sandwiches, a box of carrot sticks, and some pieces of fruit. Yum!

At one o'clock we go back to our classroom for an hour of math and 30 minutes of handwriting. Then we can choose our favorite activity. I usually draw pictures.

At a quarter till three, we go home. Our days at school are awesome!

3 Read the website again. Circle the time words.

4 Find or draw pictures about your typical school day. Then go to the Workbook to do the writing activity.

Writing strategy

Use time words *then*, *after that*, *at ten o'clock*, *in the morning* to show the sequence of events.
In the morning, I have breakfast and *then* I go to school.

98

Now I Know

1 Why do we use numbers every day? Look back through Unit 6 and write sentences with the words in the box.

> cook   music   read   shop   sports   tell the time   travel

We use numbers to remember who is winning in sports.

2 Choose a project.

Write a website about the school day in another country.

1. Find out about the school day in different countries.
2. Choose a country with an interesting school day.
3. Write a website and present it to your class.

or

Make a poster about a number.

1. Work with some friends.
2. Think of interesting facts about a number.
3. Design a poster about your number.
4. Present the poster to the class.

Read and circle for yourself.

I can identify times and prices in short dialogs.

I can extract factual details from a text.

I can ask questions about daily routines.

I can write about a typical day at school using time words.

99

7

What do we do for entertainment?

Listening
- I can identify times and prices in short dialogs.

Reading
- I can recognize the use of *because* to signal cause and effect.

Speaking
- I can describe a special event.

Writing
- I can write an ad using comparisons.

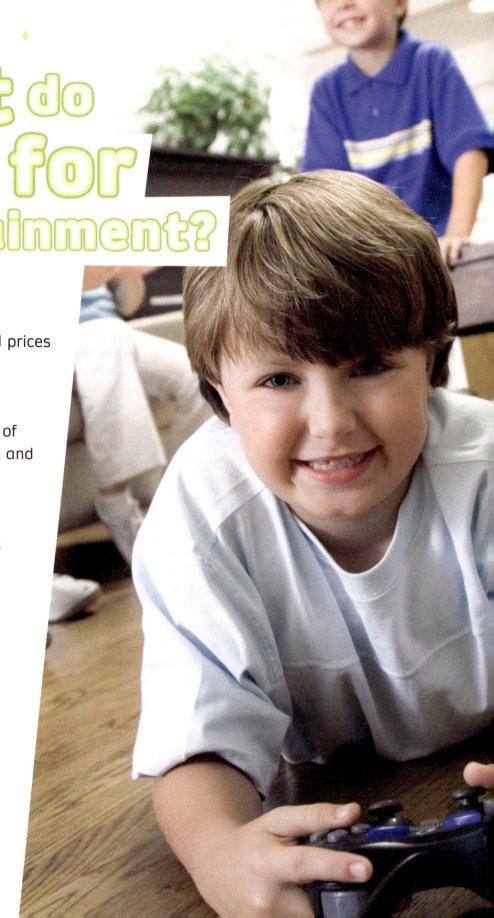

1 💬 **Look at the picture and discuss.**

1 Where are the children?
2 What can you see in the picture?
3 What are they doing? Why?

2 💬 **Think and match. Discuss with a friend.**

read   a game
play   a song
sing   a story

1 What did you do for entertainment last Saturday and Sunday / yesterday / at recess today?
2 What is good entertainment for you and your friends?

3 ▶ 7-1 BBC **Watch the video and complete the chart.**

recorder   tambourine
~~trombone~~   violin

Family	Instrument
brass	trombone
percussion	
woodwind	
strings	

101

Vocabulary 1

1 Listen and repeat.
1-51

chess · band · musician · magazine · headphones
hang out · afraid · famous · traditional · modern

2 Listen and number.
1-52

3 Write words from Activity 1. Then add more words.

Watch	Read	Listen to	Play
			chess

4 Discuss with a friend.

1 Do you know anyone famous?
2 Do you like modern music or traditional music?
3 What magazines do you read?
4 Who do you like to hang out with?

102

Pre-reading 1

Reading strategy

Identify cause and effect in a story.

1 Read the story. What was the problem?

A DANGEROUS MORNING

Karen usually listens to music on her way to school. Yesterday, she had her headphones on, as usual. She didn't look, and she almost walked into the road, in front of a car. The driver stopped suddenly, and he hit his head. He shouted at Karen and waved his arms.

2 Think and complete the chart.

| The car had to stop suddenly. | He was angry. | The driver hit his head. |

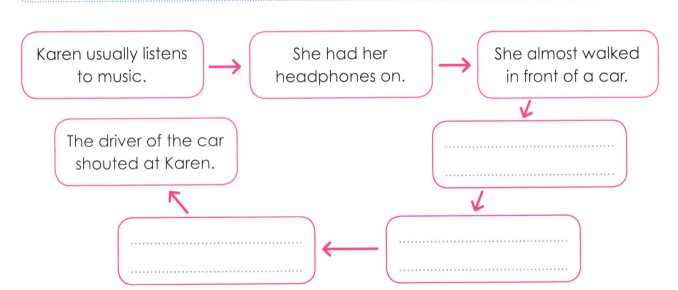

3 Complete the sentences.

The driver was angry because ....
....

The girl almost walked in front of the car because ....
....

103

Reading 1

4  Read *An Entertaining Afternoon*. Why does Mom take the children to the movies?

> **Reading strategy**
> Identify cause and effect in a story.

AN ENTERTAINING AFTERNOON

It was a rainy Sunday afternoon. Francisco's mum wanted to get the children out of the house, so she decided to take them to the cinema. Francisco and his little sister Ana were queuing with their mum to go to the cinema. Francisco was reading his **magazine** and Ana was listening to music on her **headphones** but they were getting bored. They were waiting to see *Hornet Boy*, a **modern** film adapted from a comic book.

Hornet Boy is stronger than ever and he's **afraid** of nothing. This film is in 3D and stars the **famous** actor Billy Banes.

They queued at the cinema for half an hour. But when they got to the front, they couldn't go in because there were no more tickets. Near the cinema was a board game café. They saw people playing all types of games and doing puzzles. It looked like fun, so they went inside.

5 What forms of entertainment are in the story? How often do you do them?

There was an empty table with a **chess** board, so Francisco and his family sat down. A man asked Francisco, "Do you want to play?" His face looked familiar. "Sure!" said Francisco. Then he looked carefully and realised the man was Billy Banes. Francisco sat down next to Billy Banes.

"Are you really interested in chess?" asked Francisco shyly. "Yes, I am," said Billy. "I know chess is a bit **traditional** but it really makes you think. I came here to the café today because I'm bored with playing on my computer. I want to **hang out** with real people!"

While they played, Billy and Francisco talked just like old friends. "Do you like being an actor?" Francisco asked. "Yes. I'm happy with my job but I also love music," said Billy. "One day I want to be a **musician** in a **band**."

In the end, Francisco had a great afternoon. He didn't see the film but he met his favourite actor and learnt some brilliant new chess moves.

6 Match each cause with an effect. Then make sentences with a friend. Use *so*.

CAUSE
- They wanted to get out of the house
- Francisco liked the actor Billy Banes
- There were no tickets
- One table was empty
- Billy wanted to hang out with real people

EFFECT
- he wanted to see Hornet Boy.
- he went to the board game café.
- Francisco sat down there.
- they couldn't see the movie.
- they went to the movies.

They wanted to get out of the house,
so they went to the movies.

105

Grammar 1

1   Watch Part 1 of the story video. Where's Jack? Why does the girl scream? Then read and complete.

Wait. It's OK. Don't be .... It's an MP3 player.

Oh! You're .... me.

2 Look at the grammar box and read.

Grammar

> interested in   surprised at   happy with   bored with
> afraid of   tired of   worried about

She's **interested in** comic books.
I'm **interested in** learn**ing** to play chess.
I'm **bored with** play**ing** video games.

3 Read *An Entertaining Afternoon* again and circle some of the expressions from the grammar box.

4 Read and circle.

1 Are you afraid **of** / **at** me?
2 I'm interested **with** / **in** traditional comic books.
3 She's worried **in** / **about** losing the tickets.
4 He's happy **with** / **of** his new board game.

106

5 **Discuss with a friend.**

1 What sports are you interested in?
2 What are you worried about?
3 What are you happy with?
4 What are you bored with?
5 What are you afraid of?
6 Were you surprised at any news last week?

Listening and Speaking 1

 Speaking strategy

Show agreement.

6 **Listen and check (✓) the activities.**
1-54

a  b  c  d

7 **Discuss your free time with a friend. Use the words in the box or your own ideas.**

comic books
computer games
movies
music
sports

What do you like doing in your free time?

I like listening to music.

I like music too. What music are you interested in?

I'm interested in pop music.

What's your favorite band?

I like … .

107

Vocabulary 2

1 Listen and repeat.

orchestra · cello · drum · clarinet · saxophone
trombone · trumpet · string · dream · exciting

2 Listen and number.

3 Write words from Activity 1 in the chart. Then add more instruments.

Instruments you blow	Instruments you hit	Instruments with strings
trumpet		

4 Read and cross out the wrong word.

1. violin, cello, ~~clarinet~~
2. violin, saxophone, clarinet
3. sleep, look, dream
4. amazing, exciting, boring
5. trombone, drum, trumpet
6. orchestra, cello, saxophone

5 Discuss with a friend.

1 Do you play a musical instrument? If you do, which instrument? When and where do you practice?
2 Do you think playing a musical instrument is difficult?
3 Is it a good form of entertainment?

Pre-reading 2

1 Read the article. What's the main point?

a Young people spend too much time playing video games.
b Interactive games are the best.
c Young people play video games a lot, but older people don't.

Reading strategy

Ignore unnecessary information when reading.

2 Underline the sentence in the article that is NOT about video games.

How many hours do you spend playing video games in a normal week?

A study says that many nine-year-olds play them for more than four hours a week. There are a lot of different games, including games that let you build your own world or play online with friends.

Young people play video games a lot, but older people don't. Older people spend their time on the computer watching videos or looking for information on the internet.

Reading 2

3 🎧 2-03 Read *Youth Music News*. Which information is NOT important? Check (✓)

☐ Elena is in a youth orchestra.
☐ The conductor gives the audience a message.
☐ The youth orchestra is playing in an important concert.

Reading strategy

Ignore unnecessary information when reading.

YOUTH MUSIC NEWS

The most important night of their lives!

It's almost six o'clock at the National Theater. The musicians of the San Martin Youth **Orchestra** are waiting to take their places. Five orchestras played before them. All these young people **dream** of winning the Music Festival prize.

Nine-year-old Elena is holding her **trumpet**. She feels nervous but happy that it's time to perform at last. Elena is next to her best friend, Karla, who plays the **clarinet**. They smile at each other as the conductor tells the audience to turn off their phones. They both take a deep breath and walk onto the stage.

4 💬 Ask and answer with a friend.

1 Do you sometimes play or sing in concerts?
2 Do you like to be on stage?
3 Do you like going to concerts?
4 Which musician or band would you like to see in concert?

Earlier Elena introduced me to the newest member of the orchestra, Luis. He plays the **trombone**. He said he thought it was the most difficult instrument. "Why did you decide to learn the trombone, Luis?" I asked. "I wanted a musical hobby, and I think the trombone has the most interesting sound. I play the **cello**, too. I like sports, but music is more creative."

"And why did you join the orchestra, Elena?" I asked. "I was shy and I didn't have many friends," Elena replied. "My mom told me to find a hobby and Karla suggested the orchestra. The first instrument I played was the **drum**, but the trumpet is more **exciting**. I want to learn to play the **saxophone** next! Now I have a lot of new friends, and we travel together to perform in different places. I love it!"

Elena and the San Martin Youth Orchestra won the prize. And now they are busy rehearsing for their next music festival in London, England.

5 Read and choose the sentence that is not important.

1. a Elena wants to win a prize.
   b Elena plays the trumpet.
   c The concert starts at six o'clock.

2. a Elena joined the orchestra to make friends.
   b Elena's first instrument was the drum.
   c She enjoys playing in different festivals and has a lot of new friends.

Grammar 2

1   Watch Parts 2 and 3 of the story video. Read and circle.

I think watching DVDs is **more** / **most** interesting than playing an instrument.

Well, I think it's the most exciting instrument

2 Look at the grammar box and read.

3 Read *Youth Music News* again. Circle the phrases with *more* and *most*.

Grammar

big**ger than**   **the** big**gest**

more interesting **than**   **the most** interesting

4 Complete the chart.

angrier than   louder than   more interesting than
more modern than   the happiest   the longest
the most exciting   the most famous

-er	-est	more	the most
bigger than	the biggest	more exciting than	
longer than		more traditional than	the most traditional
	the loudest		the most modern
happier than		more famous than	
	the angriest		the most interesting

112

5 Read the brochure and answer the questions.

Entertainment for Everyone at
CITY FESTIVAL

A Music for Relaxation
On Sunday, the local Yoga Center has a music meditation workshop. This is the most relaxing activity of the day.
$4.00 per person.
11:00 a.m.–4:30 p.m.

B Music for Creativity
Bring the youngest and the oldest to enjoy painting set to music.
$5.00 for materials.
9:00 a.m.–11:00 a.m.

C Comic Swap
Come and see the funniest characters and some of the world's oldest comic books. Bring your comic books to swap and sell.
$17.00 entry. All day.

D Classics at the Park
This is always a very popular part of the day. See the world famous conductor, Drefus Dudas. Sure to be the most exciting performance under the open sky.
$2.00 per person. 4:00 p.m.

1 Which is the cheapest activity?
2 Which is more expensive: painting or comic swap?
3 Which is the most relaxing activity?
4 Which activity do you think is the most interesting?

Listening and Speaking 2

6 Listen and take notes.

Name of event: *Soccer fun day*
Day / Place: *Main Stadium*
Start time / Finish time:
Things to do: *watch the charity soccer match*

Ticket price:

7 Think of an event in your town. Ask and answer with a friend.

1 What event is it?
2 What day does it take place?
3 What activities are there?
4 How much are the tickets?

113

Writing

1 Look quickly at the title. What do you think the advert is for?

2 Read the advert and check your answer to Activity 1.

THE MOST AMAZING CAR SHOW IN TOWN!

Do you love vintage cars? Come and see the city's oldest collection of traditional Model T Fords.

Are you interested in modern cars? Our exhibit is even bigger than last year. You can sit in the world's most expensive car. It's a truly incredible experience. Bring the whole family to the Downtown Motor Museum. We have food stands and competitions with fantastic prizes.

Saturday and Sunday
10 a.m. until 8 p.m.
Ticket prices (per day):
Adult $20 • Child $5 •
Family (2 adults, up to 3 children) $40.

THIS IS THE MOST EXCITING CAR SHOW OF THE DECADE!

HOW TO FIND US:
The Downtown Motor Museum is in New Street, next to the park. Parking is free all day.

3 Circle -*est*/*the most* in the advert.

4 Find or draw a picture of event you want to advertise. Then go to the Workbook to do the writing activity.

Writing strategy

Use *the ... -est/the most* to get your reader's attention.
The oldest collection of traditional Model T Fords.
The world's **most expensive** car.

Now I Know

1 **What do we do for entertainment? Look back through Unit 7 and write your answers.**

go to the movies

2 Choose a project.

Find out about entertainment in the past.

1. Work in groups.
2. Think about different forms of entertainment in the past.
3. Ask older people questions. For example, did you go to music concerts?
4. Present to the class.

or

Make a poster about a famous musician from your country.

1. Work in pairs.
2. Choose your favorite musician.
3. Create a poster with images and key facts.
4. Present your poster to the class.

Read and circle for yourself.

I can identify times and prices in short dialogs.

I can recognize the use of *because* to signal cause and effect.

I can describe a special event.

I can write an ad using comparisons.

115

8
Why is space interesting?

Listening
- I can understand how someone feels.

Reading
- I can infer information in a text.

Speaking
- I can act out a short dialog with a friend.

Writing
- I can ask questions in an email to show I am interested.

1 💬 **Look at the picture and discuss.**

1 What's the man looking at?
2 Is he in the city or the country? Why?
3 Do you sometimes do this?

2 💬 **Think and check (✓). Discuss with a friend.**

1 What's your favorite time of the day?

☐ morning ☐ afternoon
☐ evening ☐ night

2 What can you see in the sky at night from your house?
3 Which is our closest star?
4 Do you know the names of any other stars?

3 ▶️ **Watch the video. How many planets are there?**

117

Vocabulary 1

1 **Listen and repeat.**

Moon, bright, worried, cry, stick, owl, in a hurry, frightened, bump, rude

2 **Listen and number.**

3 **Read and match.**

1 Small children often cry when
2 The moon is very bright when
3 The man was in a hurry
4 You see owls with sticks when
5 People can seem rude when

a they don't say *thank you*.
b it's full.
c they're making a nest.
d they're frightened.
e to catch a train.

4 **Read and circle.**

1 It was a winter's night and the **moon** / **sun** was bright.
2 My mom is always in **slow** / **a hurry**.
3 The man on the train was **rude** / **cry**.
4 I had a **bump** / **stick** on the head.

118

5 🗨 Ask and answer with a friend.

1 Are you worried about anything now? What?
2 What are you frightened of?
3 When did you last get a bump on your head?

Pre-reading 1

1 Read the story and circle the three main characters.

Reading strategy

Identify things that have human qualities.

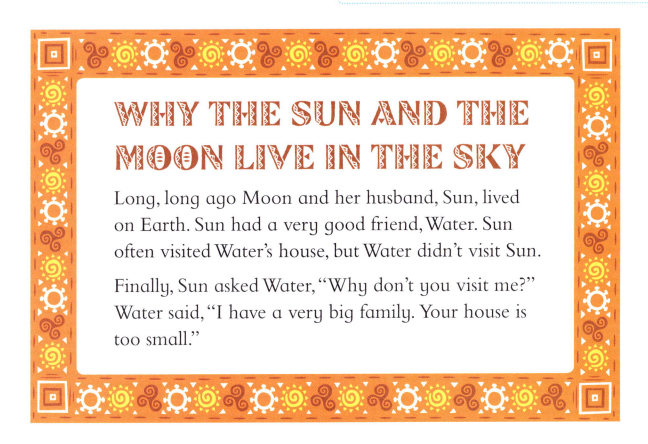

WHY THE SUN AND THE MOON LIVE IN THE SKY

Long, long ago Moon and her husband, Sun, lived on Earth. Sun had a very good friend, Water. Sun often visited Water's house, but Water didn't visit Sun.

Finally, Sun asked Water, "Why don't you visit me?" Water said, "I have a very big family. Your house is too small."

2 💡 What human qualities do Sun, Moon, and Water have?

Reading 1

3 Read *Blue Jay and the Moon*. What's Blue Jay like?

> **Reading strategy**
>
> Identify things that have human qualities.

Blue Jay and the Moon

Long, long ago **Moon** always came out at the same time, in the same place. He shone beautifully. The people of the Earth used his **bright** light to see and play.

Then one night, Moon didn't appear. "What happened?" the people asked. "The dark is frightening. We can't see! Where's Moon?" They were very **worried** and they started to **cry**.

Blue Jay was a beautiful bird with an enchanting voice. He heard the people crying and said, "Don't worry. I can go and find Moon."

On the way to Moon's house, Blue Jay saw an old man. The old man said, "Do you want to visit Moon? Remember, take a **stick** with you." But Blue Jay said, "I'm **in a hurry**." He didn't stop to talk to the old man.

At the top of some trees, Blue Jay met **Owl**. She said, "Do you want to visit Moon? Remember, be careful how you talk to him. You have to be nice." But Blue Jay didn't listen. He said, "I don't have time," and he didn't stop to talk to Owl.

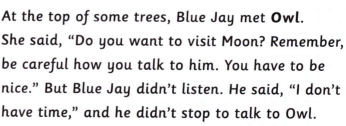

Blue Jay finally arrived at Moon's house, high in the sky. The door of the house banged open in the wind. Blue Jay flew toward the door and it closed suddenly. The door hit Blue Jay on the head.

Moon came to the door and put a stick in it to open it. "Moon! Your stupid door hit me on the head!" shouted Blue Jay, angrily. "I'm here because the people are **frightened**. Why didn't you appear in the sky tonight?"

Moon was very surprised. He said, "Please don't speak to me like that, Blue Jay." But Blue Jay went on shouting at Moon, rubbing the **bump** on his head.

Then Moon said, "People don't need me in the same place at the same time every night. I want to appear in the sky at different times and in different places. You're a **rude** bird, and you never listen, so I'm teaching you a lesson. You will always have a bump on your head and a horrible voice."

4 Think and write *Moon, Blue, Jay, old man, Owl*.

1. He's rude. — Blue Jay
2. She gives advice.
3. He wants to help with the door.
4. He's angry with Blue Jay.
5. He makes wrong decisions.
6. She lives in a tree.

5 Discuss with a friend.

1. Do you know any more stories about the Moon, the Sun, or the stars?
2. Why did people tell these stories?
3. How do we find out about the universe today?

Grammar 1

1   Watch Part 1 of the story video. Why are people frightened? Then read and complete.

I'm _____ too.

2 Look at the grammar box and read.

Grammar

It's **interesting**.   I'm **interested**.

It was **frightening**.   They were **frightened**.

The stars are **amazing**.   He's **amazed**.

The movie was **boring**.   We were **bored**.

3 Read *Blue Jay and the Moon* again and circle the *-ing* and *-ed* adjectives.

4 Read and circle.

1. The movie was **interesting** / **interested**.
2. The car journey was **bored** / **boring**.
3. My sister is **frightening** / **frightened** of the dark.
4. The view from the mountain is **amazing** / **amazed**.

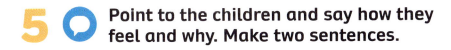

5 Point to the children and say how they feel and why. Make two sentences.

1

2

3

4

Picture 4. They are amazed. The science experiment is amazing.

Listening and Speaking 1

Speaking strategy

Shake your head to show disagreement.

6 2-08   Listen and circle.

1
   a   b

2
   a   b

3
   a   b

4
   a   b

7 2-09   Listen again and say how each person feels and why.

He's worried because …

8   Work with a friend. Look at the pictures in Activity 5 and role-play the dialogs.

You look surprised. Are you surprised?

No, I'm not surprised. I'm worried.

Why are you worried?

I'm worried because I didn't do my homework.

123

Vocabulary 2

1 **Listen and repeat.**
2-10

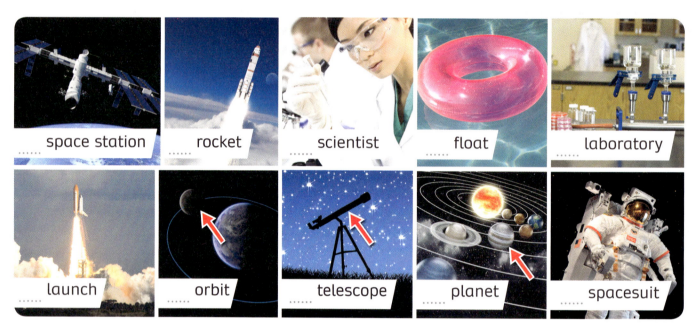

space station | rocket | scientist | float | laboratory
launch | orbit | telescope | planet | spacesuit

2 **Listen and number.**
2-11

3 **Read and write a word from Activity 1.**

1. Sticks do this in water.
2. Astronauts wear this in space.
3. This is a place where astronauts live. It orbits the Earth.
4. This is a room where scientists work.
5. We use this to look at the night sky.
6. People do this to send rockets up into space.

4 **Look at the words in Activity 1. Circle the space words.**

5 **Discuss with a friend.**

1. Can you name the planets in our solar system?
2. Can you name something that orbits the Earth?
3. Can you name something that floats?
4. Can you name a famous scientist? What did he/she study?

Pre-reading 2

1 What do you know about training to be an astronaut? What do you want to know? Complete the first two columns of the KWL chart. Then read the article.

Reading strategy
Use a KWL technique to help you understand a text.

Learning to be an ASTRONAUT		
K = What I **know**	W = What I **want** to know	L = What I **learned**
You have to study for a long time before you go into space.	What subjects do you have to study to be an astronaut?	

Learning to be an ASTRONAUT

Did you know that astronauts sometimes have other jobs first? They can be engineers, science teachers or scientists. Then they have to train to be an astronaut for two years.

The US space programme is in Houston, Texas. There the trainee astronauts study science, Maths, medicine and languages. One important language for working on the International Space Station is Russian because the Control Centre is in Russia. The trainees also practise living without gravity in special machines.

2 Read the article again and complete the third column of the KWL chart.

125

Reading 2

 Reading strategy

Use a KWL technique to help you understand a text.

3 What do you know about life on the International Space Station? What do you want to know? Make a KWL chart in your notebooks.

4 Read *Life on the International Space Station*. Did you find what you wanted to know?

Life on the INTERNATIONAL SPACE STATION

High above the Earth a group of people live and work in a moving **laboratory**. Their home travels very fast and from the window the Earth looks incredibly beautiful.

Astronauts from many countries work at the International **Space Station**. It **orbits** Earth every 90 minutes. They haven't got day and night like we have. They see sunrise and sunset 15 times a day! They also watch the weather on Earth – they can see clouds, storms and even lightning.

Astronauts began constructing the International Space Station in 1998 and they finished 13 years later. It is now big enough for seven people to work, play and sleep in. They usually live on the space station for six months.

The **scientists** on the International Space Station are very busy. They use powerful **telescopes** to study the Earth, **planets**, stars and outer space. They work on computers and check their experiments three times a day.

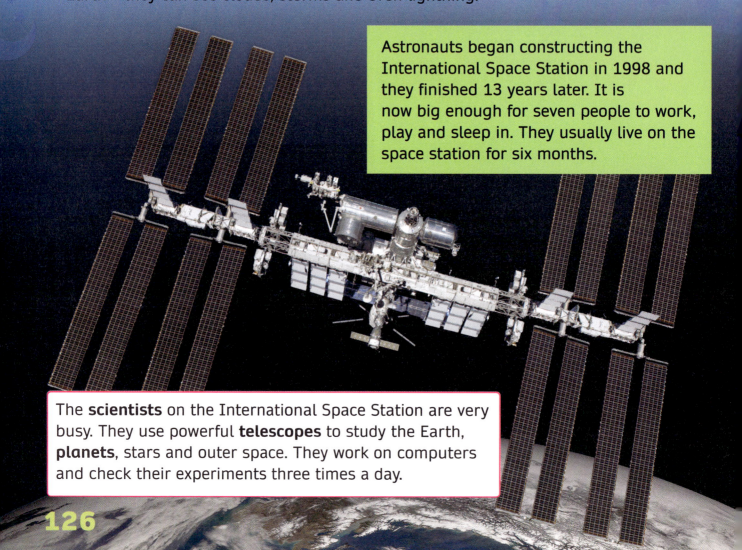

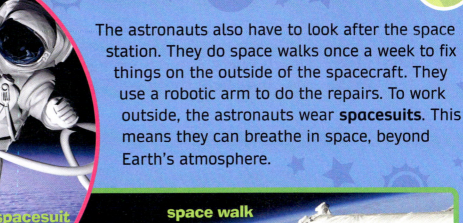

robotic arm
spacesuit
space walk

The astronauts also have to look after the space station. They do space walks once a week to fix things on the outside of the spacecraft. They use a robotic arm to do the repairs. To work outside, the astronauts wear **spacesuits**. This means they can breathe in space, beyond Earth's atmosphere.

In the past, astronauts ate strange food but these days they eat regular food, like pasta and vegetables.
The food arrives in a **rocket**, which **launches** from Earth once a month. Sleeping is difficult. Some astronauts go to sleep in the air. Others tie themselves into bed so they don't **float** around.

Staying healthy in space is important, so the astronauts exercise every day. They use special stationary bikes or running machines.

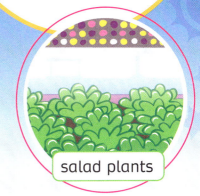

running machine

Did you know?
One experiment on the space station tests if salad plants can grow in space. Some countries are getting ready to send people to Mars, where plants can't grow.

salad plants

5 Work with a friend. Look at the pictures of these things. Then find and read the sentences with these phrases.

spacesuit   robotic arm
salad plants   space walk
running machine

6 Read the article again. Circle **T** (true) or **F** (false).

1 The International Space Station orbits Earth every 20 minutes.   T F

2 They see the sunrise 15 times a day.   T F

3 They never exercise.   T F

4 The astronauts use big telescopes to study space.   T F

Grammar 2

1   Watch Parts 2 and 3 of the story video. What can the clues help them do? Then read and complete.

How .... do we have quests? I love a good quest!

2 Read the grammar box and circle. Then compare answers with a friend.

> **Grammar**
>
> **Once** means one time and **twice** means two times.
>
> 1 **How often does** the Moon orbit the Earth?
>
>   The Moon orbits the Earth **once a month** / **twice a day**.
>
> 2 **How often does** the Earth orbit the Sun?
>
>   The Earth orbits the Sun **three times a year** / **once a year.**
>
> 3 **How often do** the astronauts see the sunrise?
>
>   They see the sunrise **every 20 minutes** / **every 90 minutes.**

3 Read *Life on the International Space Station* again. Circle the phrases that tell you how often something happens.

4 Read and complete.

1 .... an hour = every 30 minutes
2 once an hour = every 60 minutes
3 twice a day = every 12 hours
4 every Friday = ... a week
5 four times a month = every week

6 .... a month = every two weeks
7 once a month = every four weeks
8 three times a year = every four months
9 .... a year = every six months

Listening and Speaking 2

5 Listen and check (✓).

Ken

1
☐ sometimes
☐ every day

2
☐ once a week
☐ once a month

3
☐ twice a month
☐ twice a week

Kerry

1
☐ three times a year
☐ once a year

2
☐ once a week
☐ twice a month

3
☐ every Friday
☐ every day

6 Ask and answer with a friend.

How often do you go camping?   Once a year.

Writing

1 Read Dan's email to an astronaut. Where did Sophie send an email to Dan's class from?

2 Ask and answer.

1. Who's writing the email?
2. Who's he writing to?
3. Where's she?

To: Sophie Astronaut

Subject: How do you sleep in space?

Dear Sophie,

Thank you for emailing my class from the International Space Station. I think space is really interesting.

I read that you have day and night 15 times a day. The sky is always light and then dark. Do you need to wear sunglasses? It's amazing that you can see the Earth from space, and you can see storms and lightning from above. Can you see the stars, too? Can you see the Big Dipper and Little Dipper? What does the Moon look like from space?

I am interested in life in space, and I have some questions: How do you sleep when there is no gravity? Are you bored with eating the same food all the time? What do you miss most about Earth? Also, how often do you talk to your family?

Looking forward to hearing from you.

Dan
3B
Southside Elementary

---

3 Read the email again. Find and circle the questions Dan asks.

4 Think of questions you want to ask an astronaut. Then go to the Workbook to do the writing activity.

Writing strategy

Ask questions in an email to show that you're interested. *What does the Moon look like from space?*

130

Now I Know

1 Why is space interesting? Look back through Unit 8 and write more answers.

Because life in space is different from life on Earth.

2 Choose a project.

Research a famous astronaut.

1. Work in groups of three. Choose an astronaut.
2. Think of the things you want to know before you start your research. Do a KWL chart.
3. Do the research using the library or the internet.
4. Make a poster and prepare to present your astronaut.
5. Give a presentation to the class.

or

Do a presentation on the Moon.

1. Work in groups. Think about how the Moon looks.
2. Research the phases of the Moon.
3. Make a model or models of the Moon, or make a poster about the Moon with images and key words.
4. Display the model or poster in the classroom.

Read and circle for yourself.

I can understand how someone feels.

I can infer information in a text.

I can act out a short dialog with a friend.

I can ask questions in an email to show I am interested.

131

How are homes different?

Listening
- I can understand most details in conversations about where people live.

Reading
- I can understand the main ideas in a short story about homes.

Speaking
- I can role-play a short dialog with a friend.

Writing
- I can connect ideas to describe my perfect home.

1 💬 **Look at the picture and discuss.**

1 What can you see in the picture?
2 Where do these people live?
3 Would you like to live here?

2 Look at the list. Number the things in order from very important (1) to not important (9).

bookcase ..... kitchen ..... fridge .....
window ..... bed ..... stove .....
bathroom ..... TV ..... chair .....

3 Imagine you live in a place with very different weather. Do your answers to Activity 2 change?

4 ▶ 9-1 **Watch the video. Check (✓) the things you see.**

☐ a house in a tree
☐ a house in a desert
☐ a house on the water
☐ a house made of mud and straw
☐ a house on a boat

133

Vocabulary 1

1 **Listen and repeat.**

roof · balcony · attic · view · wood
stone · sweep · build · steep · flat

2 **Listen and number.**

3 **Read and cross out the wrong word.**

1 The walls of my house are made of **stone** / ~~flat~~ / **wood**.
2 The street outside my house is very **sweep** / **flat** / **steep**.
3 There's a beautiful view from the **balcony** / **window** / **build**.
4 Let's go on the **view** / **balcony** / **roof** and sit in the sun.
5 I should sweep the **balcony** / **floor** / **steep** today.
6 You'll find these at the top of the house in the **roof** / **stone** / **attic**.

4 **Discuss with a friend.**

1 Is your home an apartment or a house?
2 Are the walls made of stone or wood?
3 Does it have a flat or steep roof?
4 Does your home have an attic/a yard/a balcony?
5 What's the view from your bedroom window?

134

Pre-reading 1

1 Read the first part of a story. Choose the best summary.

Reading strategy

Write a summary to help you remember what you read.

A good summary is short. It includes the most important things in the story.

1. Mrs Mouse and her children lived in a nice house.
2. Mrs Mouse lived with her children in a pretty stone house with a roof made of wood and a lot of yellow and blue flowers in the garden.
3. The house was very pretty.

Mrs Mouse lived with her children in a little house in the country. It was made of stone, with a roof made of wood, and there were a lot of flowers in the front garden. It was very pretty.

2 Read the next part of the story and write a summary.

But the children grew and grew. When the family had dinner, two of the children had to sit on the cupboards because there wasn't space at the table. When they went to sleep, one little mouse had to sleep under the bed on the floor. "Mum, we need a bigger house," they said.

Reading 1

Reading strategy

Write a summary to help you remember what you read.

3 🎧 2-16 Read *The Perfect Home*. Match the summaries to the parts 1–3.

a He builds a house with a flat roof in the mountains. ☐

b Brad the Rabbit lives in the city, but he wants a view of the countryside. ☐

c In winter, he doesn't sweep the snow off his roof. The snow breaks his roof. ☐

THE PERFECT HOME

❶ Brad the Rabbit sat on his **flat roof** and looked at the **view** of the city. "I love my house," he thought. "But cities are ugly. I'd like to have a view of the countryside!"

❷ He went to the mountains. "It's so pretty!" he thought. "I'd like to live here." He **built** a house. All the other houses in the neighbourhood had a **steep** roof, a **balcony** and a bedroom in the **attic**. But his had a flat roof, like his house in the city. "It's perfect!" he said.

❸ In autumn, Brad enjoyed the view of the mountains. But in winter it started to snow. It snowed for two weeks. The snow fell off the steep roofs of the other houses but there was lots of snow on Brad's roof.
"You should **sweep** the snow off your roof," said his neighbour. But it was cold outside. Brad stayed inside, in front of the fire.
One day, Brad heard a noise. "Crack!" It was the roof! "Help!" he said as he ran out of his house. Behind him, the snow and the roof fell into the rooms below.

4 After that, Brad didn't want to live in a snowy place. He went to a forest. "The trees are very beautiful," he thought. "I'd like to live here."
He built a house. All the other houses in the neighbourhood were made of **stone**. But his house was made of **wood**, like his house in the city. "It's perfect!" he thought.
In spring, Brad enjoyed the view of the forest. But in summer, the weather was hotter and the forest was drier.

5 One day, Brad heard a noise. "Roar!" It was a forest fire!
"Help!" said Brad as he ran out of his house. Behind him, the fire burnt everything made of wood. His beautiful forest home was a ruin.

6 Brad's neighbour saw him. "Would you like to come to my house?" she asked. "It didn't burn because it's made of stone."
"Sorry, I can't," said Brad. "I have to go back to my old house. It's safe and it's got a wonderful view of the city. It's perfect!"

4 Write summaries for parts 4–6 of the story.

5 Answer the questions. Use the summaries from Activities 3 and 4 to help you find the correct place in the story.

1. What were the other houses in the forest made of?
2. What did the other houses in the mountains have in their attics?
3. In which season did Brad enjoy the view of the forest?

6 Discuss with a friend.

1. Is there snow in your country in winter? What problems are there when there's a lot of snow?
2. Are there sometimes forest fires in your country? Do they ever burn people's homes?

137

Grammar 1

1 Watch Part 1 of the story video. What has happened to the streets?

I'd like to live on a tidier street!

2 Look at the grammar box and read.

> **Grammar**
>
> **Would you like to visit** Hong Kong?
>
> Yes, I **would like to visit** Hong Kong.
>
> No, I **wouldn't like to visit** Hong Kong.
>
> Would he like to meet an alien?
>
> Yes, he**'d like to meet** an alien.
>
> No, he **wouldn't like to meet** an alien.

3 Read *The Perfect Home* again and circle sentences with *I'd like* or *would you like.*

4 Look at the pictures and then write the answers.

hammock

four-poster bed

tent

Where would you like to sleep? Why? _____

Where wouldn't you like to sleep? Why? _____

138

5 Read and complete. Write *People* or *Things*.

....

Dua's roof   the roof **of the house**
the doctor's name   the name **of the spaceship**

There was a lot of snow on **Brad's** roof.
The floor **of the attic** is dirty!

6 Choose pairs of words from the box and make phrases with *'s* or *of*.

car   Dad   friend   floor   Grandma
house   roof   tent   walls   wheels

the floor of the tent

Dad's car

Speaking

7 💡 Imagine your perfect life when you're older. Think about these things. Then ask and answer with a friend.

- your home
- your children
- your friends
- your job
- your hobbies
- your vacations
- your pets
- your neighborhood

> 💬 **Speaking strategy**
>
> Respect the opinions of others.

Would you like to have children?

Yes, I would. I'd like to have two children. How about you?

No, I wouldn't. I would like to have a lot of pets.

Vocabulary 2

1 **Listen and repeat.**

narrow | wide | concrete | bricks | metal
plastic | move | stairs | elevator | basement

2 **Listen and number.**

3 Write words from Activity 1 in the chart.

Materials	Things in a building	Things you do
bricks,		

4 **Discuss with a friend.**

1. Are the streets in old neighborhoods wide or narrow? What about modern neighborhoods? Why?
2. Which material is usually better for a home in a hot, sunny place: bricks or metal? Why?
3. When you can choose, do you usually take the stairs or the elevator? Why?

Pre-reading 2

1 💡 Look, read, and compare.

1. What's the same about the two places?
2. Which place has more underground homes?
3. Which homes are easier to build?

> **Reading strategy**
>
> Compare the things or people in a text.

COOBER PEDY AUSTRALIA

This Australian town is famous for its underground homes. More than 1,500 families live underground, and some of the homes are 60 years old or more. When people want a bigger bedroom, they just dig out the rock. They stop when the room is the right size.

DIETIKON SWITZERLAND

There are nine underground homes around a small lake in this town in Switzerland. The homes have an interesting, modern design, but they aren't easy to build. First, you have to make the shape of the rooms with metal. Next, you put concrete on the metal. Then you put earth and grass on the top.

2 Look at the pictures on the next page and guess. Which of the homes are …

1. modern?
2. old?
3. on water?
4. narrow?
5. tall?
6. in Amsterdam?

3 Which home on the next page do you prefer?

141

Reading 2

4 🎧 2-19 Read *Where We Live: Amsterdam*. Check your answers from Activity 2.

> **Reading strategy**
>
> Compare the things or people in a text.

Where We Live: Amsterdam

Amsterdam

A lot of people want to live and work in Amsterdam, but there isn't much land for homes. Where do people live?

1
I live in an apartment on the twenty-first floor of a skyscraper. Skyscrapers are really useful in cities because you can have a lot of homes on a small piece of land. My building is made of **concrete** and **metal**, and it looks very modern.
The best thing about it is the view. The worst thing is taking the **stairs** when the **elevator** breaks down!

Merel

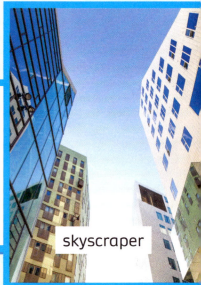
skyscraper

5 Read the article again and answer the questions.

1. Name four materials used to construct the different homes.
2. What is the worst thing about living in a skyscraper?
3. How old is the house made of bricks?
4. How many canals are there in Amsterdam?

6 💬 Discuss with a friend.

1. Think about each home in the text. Why is it useful in a place like Amsterdam?
2. Are there homes like these in your city or neighborhood?
3. Would you like to live in these homes? Why? / Why not?

142

2

My home is on a lake. It floats on the water, but it isn't a boat. It's a new kind of house, made of metal and **plastic**. It's perfect for Amsterdam because there's a lot of water here, but not much land. There's a kitchen in the **basement**, a living room on the first floor, and bedrooms on the second floor. We can't keep our car next to the house, but we mostly use our boat. Shopping by boat is fun!

Max

floating house

3

I live downtown, in a house made of **bricks**. It's about 350 years old, and it's very, very **narrow**. We can't carry big furniture upstairs because the stairs are too small. When we **moved** here, we had to bring things in through the windows! But our house is **wider** at the back than at the front, and it's on four floors, so it's really very comfortable. Living downtown is great!

Isabel

4

My home is a houseboat on a canal. There are 165 canals in Amsterdam, so there's a lot of space for houseboats. We usually keep ours in the same place, but because it's made of wood, it sometimes has to go to the shipyard for repairs. It has all the same things as a traditional home: a shower, a toilet, a TV. But it's better than a house because I have swans as neighbors!

Lars

swans

a houseboat

a canal

land

Grammar 2

1   Watch Part 2 of the story video. Which floor does the Smogator go to at the end?

2 Read the grammar box and complete the chart.

Grammar

1st	**first**	8th	**eighth**	20th	**twentieth**
2nd	**second**	9th	**ninth**	21st	**twenty-first**
3rd	**third**	10th	**tenth**	22nd	_____
4th	**fourth**	11th	**eleventh**	23rd	**twenty-third**
5th	**fifth**	12th	**twelfth**	24th	_____
6th	**sixth**	13th	**thirteenth**	30th	**thirtieth**
7th	_____	14th	_____		

3 Read *Where We Live: Amsterdam* again and complete.

1 Merel lives on the _____ floor.
2 Max's bedroom is on the _____ floor.

4 Write three more numbers in each list.

1 ninth, tenth, _____, _____, _____
2 twenty-fourth, twenty-fifth, _____, _____, _____
3 twenty-third, twenty-second, _____, _____, _____

144

5 💬 Imagine you live in a very tall apartment block. Choose a floor and discuss with a friend.

> Do you live on the fourth floor?

> No, I don't. I live above the fourth floor. I live on the tenth floor.

Listening

6 🎧 2-20 Listen to a radio program: *Homes Around the World*. Number the questions and complete the answers.

☐ Why are the buildings so tall? Because they were _____ when there were attacks.

☐ What's your building made of? It's made of _____ .

☐ Who do you live with? My mom, my dad, and my _____ .

☒ 1 Where do you live? In a city in the *desert* .

☐ When did your family move here? A very _____ time ago.

☐ Which floor do you live on? On the _____ floor.

7 Look at the questions in Activity 6. Read and match.

Wh- questions

1	when	a	a place	
2	where	b	a time	
3	who	c	a reason	
4	what	d	a thing	
5	why	e	a choice	
6	which	f	a person	

What are the walls made of?
Who do you live with?
Which subjects **do** you do at school?
Where does your uncle live?
Why were tall buildings safer?
When did Ahmed move to Shibam?

8   Watch Part 3 of the story video. Where's the swimming pool?

145

Writing

1 Javi is writing about his perfect home. Look at the picture and guess the answers to questions 1–7.

1. Where is it?
2. What kind of home is it? Is it a house? An apartment? A skyscraper?
3. What's it like? Is it big or small? Is it modern or traditional?
4. What's it made of?
5. Does it have a basement, balcony, or attic?
6. Where does Javi eat?
7. What's his bedroom like?

2 Read the blog and check your answers.

MY PERFECT HOME
BY JAVI KANO

My perfect home is my hometown. I don't want to move to a different place, because all my friends live here. I'd like to have a big, modern house made of wood and stone. It should have ten rooms or more, and a swimming pool in the basement, too. I'd like to go swimming every afternoon after school!

I'd like to eat in a beautiful dining room on the first floor in winter, and on the balcony on the second floor in the summer. I'd like to sleep in a big bedroom in the attic, with a dinosaur blanket on the bed. I'd also like to have a view of the ocean from my bedroom window.

What about you? What's your perfect home?

3 Read the blog again. Find and circle *too* and *also*.

4 Find or draw pictures of your perfect home. Then go to the Workbook to do the writing activity.

✏️ Writing strategy

Use *too* and *also* to connect ideas in your writing.
I'd *also* like to have a view.

146

Now I Know

1 How are homes different? Look back through Unit 9 and complete the sentences.

1 Homes can be made from ...

2 Skyscrapers have ...

3 People live on water because ...

4 Homes can be modern or ...

2 Choose a project.

Role-play a dialog about your perfect home.

1 Compare your perfect homes from Writing Activity 4 with a friend.
2 Discuss the different homes.
3 Prepare and perform a dialog in class.

or

Make a poster about a home in another country.

1 Find out about interesting homes in different countries.
2 Choose or draw pictures of the most interesting home. Then write.
3 Show your poster to the class.

Read and circle for yourself.

I can understand most details in conversations about where people live.

I can role-play a short dialog with a friend.

I can understand the main ideas in a short story about homes.

I can connect ideas to describe my perfect home.

147

How do we take care of our body?

Listening
- I can understand most details in conversations about everyday topics.

Reading
- I can scan a text to find specific information.

Speaking
- I can role-play conversations with a friend.

Writing
- I can use appropriate greetings and closings when writing personal messages.

1 💬 **Look at the picture and discuss.**

1 What are the children doing?
2 What are they wearing? Why?
3 Would you like to play this sport? Why? / Why not?

2 💬 **Discuss with a friend.**

1 Which sports are good for your body? How?
2 Which sports can be bad for your body? How? What bad things can happen?
3 What can you do to stay safe when you play or do them?

3 BBC **Watch the video. Answer the questions.**

1 What do the children want to be?
2 Where do they go?
3 What does the boy like doing?
4 How long has Natalie been a GP?
5 What do the children check?

149

Vocabulary 1

1 **Listen and repeat.**

stomach | back | neck | shoulder | fever
bandage | take medicine | rest | pale | sick

2 **Listen and number.**

3 **Read and cross out the wrong word.**

1 Be careful! There's a bee on your **shoulder** / ~~pale~~ / **neck**.
2 When you're sick, you should **rest** / **take some medicine** / **back**.
3 At night, I usually sleep on my **back** / **stomach** / **fever**.
4 She's very **pale** / **stomach** / **sick** today.
5 Put a bandage on your **back** / **shoulder** / **rest**.

4 **Look at the words in Activity 1 and sort.**

Parts of the body	Sickness

150

5 💬 Discuss with a friend.

1 What do you usually do when you are sick with a fever?
2 Do you sometimes have to take medicine? What color is it? Does it taste nice?
3 Did you ever have to wear a bandage? On which part of your body?

Pre-reading 1

1 Read the first part of a story. Imagine how the people felt. Read and match.

> **📖 Reading strategy**
>
> When you read, imagine how the characters in the story feel.

1 When Fran won the game, she felt
2 When Fran made a mistake in the game, she felt
3 When Fran said, "Not now, Dad. Maybe later." her father felt

a angry.
b happy.
c surprised.

"Yes!" said Fran. "I won again!" *Alien Attack* was her favorite video game, and she played it for hours every day. She was very good at it.
She started the game again. But before it finished, her father came into her bedroom, and she made a silly mistake. She sighed.
"Your dinner is ready," he said. "Come downstairs and eat."
Fran didn't feel hungry, and she didn't want to stop her game.
"Not now, Dad. Maybe later."

2 💡 Now look at the pictures in the story on the next page. How do you think the people feel?

Reading 1

3 Read *Doctor Martina*. Check your answers from Activity 2.

Reading strategy

When you read, imagine how the characters in the story feel.

"I'm the doctor in our school play next month," said Martina to her Grandpa as they crossed the little river in the woods. "Would you like to come and watch?"
"Of course!" said Grandpa. "I always love your plays!"
Grandpa stopped walking and pointed at a beautiful bird on a tree above the river. "Look! A kingfisher!" he said quietly. He moved slowly towards it with his camera. But his foot hit a rock, and he fell. The ground was steep and rocky, and he went a long way down.

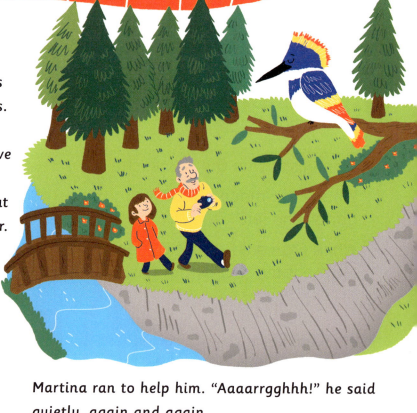

Martina ran to help him. "Aaaarrgghhh!" he said quietly, again and again.
"What's wrong, Grandpa?" Martina asked.
"My leg hurts … and my **shoulder**. And my **back**, and my head, and my **stomach** … Aaarrghh!"
There was blood on his leg, and his face was very **pale**.
"Oh, no, Grandpa! You need an ambulance," said Martina. She called 911 on Grandpa's phone. She called her parents, too.
She looked again at Grandpa's leg. She needed to stop the blood. In the play, she used **bandages**, but she didn't have any. "I know!" she thought. "I can use Grandpa's scarf." She took it from his **neck** and put it around his leg. Then she took off her coat and put it on top of Grandpa.

152

Her parents and the ambulance arrived at the same time, and soon Grandpa was on the way to the hospital. Later, Martina and her parents talked to Grandpa's doctor. "He didn't lose too much blood," the doctor said. "The scarf around his leg helped a lot. Good job! But he's very **sick**. He has a broken leg, a **fever**, and a bad headache. He needs to **rest** here and **take** the right **medicine**."

In the school play the next month, Martina felt sad because Grandpa wasn't with her parents in the audience. "I hope he can leave the hospital soon," she thought. When the play finished, the audience clapped, and someone waved a crutch in the air. Martina looked at the person's face. It was Grandpa!
"Were you surprised?" he laughed later. "I was bored with seeing the hospital doctors. I wanted to see Doctor Martina – the best doctor ever!"

4 Circle **T** (true) or **F** (false). Correct the false sentences.

1 Grandpa wants to watch Martina's play. T F
2 Grandpa falls and Martina sees blood on his face. T F
3 Martina uses a bandage to stop the blood. T F
4 Grandpa is sick with a fever. T F
5 Martina feels happy in the school play. T F

5 Answer the questions with a friend.

1 How did Martina feel in different parts of the story?
2 Why did Martina put a scarf around Grandpa's leg? And why did she put her coat on him?
3 What useful things can people do before an ambulance comes?
4 Did you ever go to the hospital?

153

Grammar 1

1   Watch Part 1 of the story video. Why are the people sick? Then read and complete.

.... the matter with you?

2 Look at the grammar box and read.

> **Grammar**
>
> **What's** the matter? **What's** wrong?
>
> **I'm** sick/fine.
> **I have** a stomachache/fever/broken arm.
> My leg **hurts**.

3 Read *Doctor Martina* again and answer.

1 What question does Martina ask Grandpa after he falls?
2 Which parts of Grandpa's body hurt after he falls?

4 Ask and answer with a friend. Find the picture.

   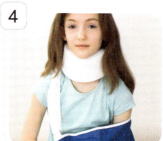

What's wrong?   I have a backache.   That's picture 3.

154

5 Imagine you or a friend are sick. What do you have to do? Ask and answer. Then tell the class.

I have a stomachache. **I have to** drink lots of water.

He has a broken arm. **He has to** have an x-ray.

She has a fever. **She has to** drink water and take some medicine.

What's the matter?

I hurt my leg. The doctor says I have to rest.

Listening and Speaking 1

6 2-24 Number the dialog in order. Then listen and check.

☐ **Doctor:** Let's look inside your ear ... Oh, yes, I can see the problem.
☐ **Sam:** I have an earache. My left ear really hurts.
☐ **Doctor:** Yes. It's purple. Don't move, and I can take it out for you ... Yes, here you are.
☐ **Sam:** A doll's shoe?!
☐ **Doctor:** No, you aren't. You're fine, but you have a doll's shoe in your ear.
☐ **Sam:** Am I very sick, Doctor?
☑ 1 **Doctor:** Hello, Sam. What's the matter?

7 Work with a friend. Role-play conversations at the doctor's.

What's wrong?

Let's look inside your mouth.

My mouth hurts!

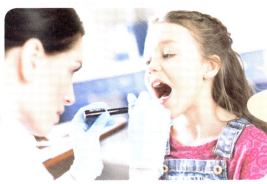

155

Vocabulary 2

1 **Listen and repeat.**

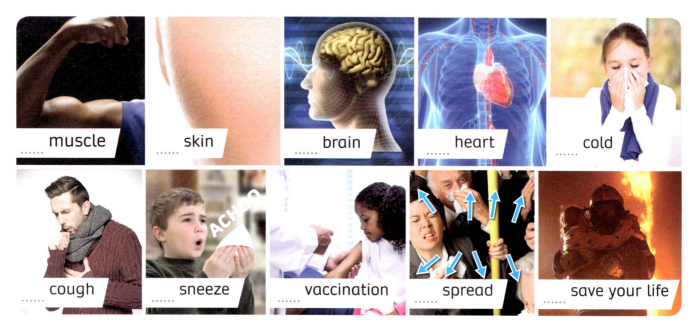

muscle · skin · brain · heart · cold
cough · sneeze · vaccination · spread · save your life

2 **Listen and number.**

3 **Read and match.**

1 Your heart   a help move other parts of your body.
2 Your skin   b pushes your blood around your body.
3 Your muscles   c is inside your head, and it's your body's computer.
4 Vaccinations   d is on the outside of your body.
5 Your brain   e can save your life.

4 **Complete the sentences with words from Activity 1.**

Flu can be a serious illness, you can also suffer from .... and .... Coughs and colds can .... if you don't cover your mouth.

156

Pre-reading 2

Reading strategy

Use information in the text to help you understand unknown words.

1 Read an extract from a leaflet. Circle the correct title for the leaflet.

1 The chemicals in our bodies
2 How to take care of your body when you exercise
3 Exercise: Why is it good for us?

Exercise can make you a happier person. When you exercise, your body makes chemicals called endorphins. Because of these endorphins, your body doesn't hurt very much when you exercise. And the endorphins also make you feel happy.

2 Circle the word *endorphins* in the leaflet. Read the words before and after *endorphins*. Then circle the best answer.

1 Endorphins are
   a parts of your body.　　b chemicals in your body.

2 When there are endorphins in your body,
   a you feel happier.　　b your body hurts more.

3 Read the leaflet on the next page. What's a germ? Which part of the leaflet tells you this?

157

Reading 2

4 Read *Say NO to Germs*. Check your answers from Activity 3.

> **Reading strategy**
>
> Use information in the text to help you understand unknown words.

Say NO to Germs

Your body is amazing. All its different parts – bones, **muscles**, **skin**, blood, **brain**, **heart**, stomach, lungs – work together to keep you alive. But diseases stop your body from working in the right way. When you've got a disease, your body has got a more difficult job.

You get diseases for lots of different reasons but one important reason is germs. Germs are very small living things. They go into your body through your mouth, nose, eyes or skin, and then they start to attack you. Some give you a **cold**, a cough or a fever. Others can kill you.

Everyone wants to stay healthy. But what should you do to protect yourself and others from germs?

1 Wash your hands

You should always wash your hands with soap after you go to the bathroom. When you don't do this, there are germs on your hands. When you touch your mouth, or your desk, or your friend's hand, you leave germs on them. That's how lots of diseases spread from one person to another.

5 Find the blue words in the leaflet. Read the words before and after them. Then circle **T** (true) or **F** (false).

1 When people die, they are alive.   T   F
2 Diseases make you sick.   T   F
3 A reason is the answer to the question "Why?"   T   F
4 If something kills someone, it saves their life.   T   F

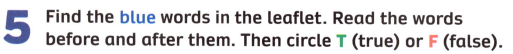

158

2 Cover your mouth

When you **cough** or **sneeze**, germs from your body go into the air. You should always put something in front of your nose and mouth to catch the germs: your arm or hand, a handkerchief or a face mask. When you don't do this, the germs go a long way. Then other people breathe them into their lungs.

3 Only drink clean water

You shouldn't drink water from rivers or lakes, because it's got lots of germs in it. Dirty water spreads lots of diseases.

4 Only eat safe food

Germs grow on meat and other food when it isn't in the fridge. You have to look after food carefully, or it can give you diseases.

5 Have vaccinations

Vaccinations sometimes hurt but they protect you from diseases when germs try to attack your body. Doctors think that vaccinations **save the lives** of two or three million people every year.

6 Discuss with a friend.

1. Can you see germs?
2. What do you usually do when you cough or sneeze? Do you spread lots of germs this way?
3. Do you ever have vaccinations? Who gives them to you? How do you feel about them? Why?
4. Why do more children die of diseases in poor countries than in rich countries? What changes can help to keep more children alive?

159

Grammar 2

1   Watch Part 2 of the story video. Where do Kim and The Doctor go? Why? Then read and complete.

2 Look at the grammar box and read.

Why .... I stay here? I want to come with you.

Grammar

You **should** go.
Jack **shouldn't** come with us.
What should we do? We **should** help them.
Should we look for the medicine?
Yes, we **should**.
No, we **shouldn't**.

3 Read *Say NO to Germs* again and circle the sentences with *should* and *shouldn't*.

4 What should you do to stay healthy? Look at the pictures and complete.

1 I .... wear a heavy backpack.
2 I .... go running.
3 .... you drink soda? No, I ....
4 .... you have vaccinations? Yes, I ....

5 Read and complete. Write *Person* or *Thing*.

....

Someone should get the medicine.
Everyone was sick.

....

I can't do **everything**.
We should do **something**.

160

6 Complete and follow the instructions. Then give similar instructions to a friend.

1 Name every _one_ in your family.
2 Name some _____ in your bedroom.
3 Name some _____ who's very tall.
4 Name every _____ on your desk.

Listening and Speaking 2

7 Who says these things? Listen and write J (Joe) or R (Rachel).

1 _R_ **You should** try it!
2 ___ **Why don't you** come to soccer practice with me?
3 ___ **I really don't want** to play soccer again.
4 ___ **Maybe you should** play tennis or badminton.
5 ___ **Why don't you try** something like kayaking?
6 ___ **Maybe I should** talk to my mom about dancing.

> **Speaking strategy**
> Show respect by making suggestions politely.

8 Role-play these conversations with a friend. Use the words in bold in Activity 7 to help you.

1 I eat a lot of candy every day, but I know it's bad for me. How can I stop?
2 Someone wants to buy the school sports field. Should we say yes and buy other things for the school with the money?

What's the matter?

Well, I eat a lot of candy every day, but …

9 Watch Part 3 of the story video. What does Jack say that they should do?

161

Writing

1 Ada is in hospital with a broken leg. Her Grandma writes her a letter. Look at the letter. Where's Ada's Grandma?

2 Now read the letter and answer.

1 How did Ada break her leg?
2 What advice does Ada's Grandma give her?
3 How long does Ada have to stay in hospital for?

Dear Ada,

How are you? I am on vacation in France so I'm sorry I can't visit you. I spoke to your mom yesterday and she told me you are going to be in hospital for a week. You poor girl!

I hope you are doing OK and your leg is getting better. You were unlucky to break your leg, it sounds like you fell off your bike badly.

You should rest and you should listen to the doctors and nurses. You shouldn't go to bed too late. You should eat lots of healthy food.

I can't wait to see you when I return from France.

Be brave and get well soon.

Love from

Grandma

3 Read the letter again. Circle the beginning and ending.

4 Find or draw pictures of a doctor giving advice. Then go to the Workbook to do the writing activity.

Writing strategy

When you write a letter or an email, begin with *Dear* and the name of the person that you are writing to. End with *Best wishes* (or *Love from* if you know the person very well) and your name.

162

Now I Know

1 **How do we take care of our body? Look back through Unit 10 and complete the sentences.**

1 When we're sick, we should ....
2 When we need to go to the hospital, we should ....
3 To stay healthy, we should ....

2 Choose a project.

Give a presentation about health.

1 Work with a friend. Make a list of ideas for being healthier.
2 Choose the three most interesting ideas.
3 Plan a presentation about these ideas. Say what we should do, and why this can make us healthier.
4 Give your presentation to the class.

or

Make a poster about a disease.

1 Think of a disease and do some research.
2 Make a poster with pictures and key words about the disease.
3 Write in which parts of the world people get it, what health problems people have and what they can do to feel better.
4 Show your poster to the class.

Read and circle for yourself.

I can understand most details in conversations about everyday topics.

I can scan a text to find specific information.

I can role-play conversations with a friend.

I can use appropriate greetings and closings when writing personal messages.

11
Why is Antarctica special?

Listening
- I can identify key details in factual conversations.

Reading
- I can understand the main points in descriptive texts about animals.

Speaking
- I can role-play a short dialog with a friend.

Writing
- I can write factual descriptions of animals.

1 Look at the picture and discuss.

1 What can you see?
2 What's the weather like?
3 What animals are there?
4 What's the man doing?

2 Discuss with a friend.

1 What's your favorite weather? Do you prefer hot weather or cold weather?
2 Do you like snow? Does it snow in your country? How long for?
3 Why do you think Antarctica is called the cleanest place on Earth?
4 Do people live in Antarctica? Why? / Why not?

3 Watch the video. Answer the questions.

1 What's Antarctica like?
2 What do the whales eat?

165

Vocabulary 1

1 Listen and repeat.

South Pole · penguin · expedition · temperature
degrees · ice · continent · freezing
crack · deep

2 Listen and number.

3 Read and write a word from Activity 1.

1. When people travel a long way to explore an area.
2. Water turns to this when the temperature is below zero.
3. This tells us how hot or cold it is.
4. You see this when ice is breaking.
5. A big piece of land made up of different countries.
6. When you go far out into the ocean, the water reaches far down.
7. When you are very, very cold.
8. This is a black and white bird that lives in Antarctica.

4 Discuss with a friend.

1 Antarctica has the South Pole. Are there any other poles?
2 Can you name all of the continents?
3 What's the coldest temperature in your country? And the hottest?
4 What animals live in Antarctica?

Pre-reading 1

1 **Read the beginning of a diary. Think about the questions as you read.**

> **Reading strategy**
>
> Check your understanding as you read.

1 What are the scientists doing?
2 Does she work alone?
3 Can you find a word that means the same as *meteorite*?
4 Why is it important not to sweat?

Today is the start of my second week working on the Antarctic Meteorite Programme. The team all come from different countries, but we love working together.
Yesterday was an exciting day. We got ready to look for space rocks, as we do every morning. We have to put on special clothes, but not too many. We walk a lot when we are looking for meteorites, and we get hot. But we have to be careful not to sweat. In the freezing temperatures of Antarctica, it can be very dangerous to have wet clothes. It's because your body loses heat much more quickly when your clothes are wet.

2 **Compare your answers to the questions in Activity 1 with a friend.**

167

Reading 1

3 🎧 2-31 Read *An Extraordinary Expedition*. Where's the expedition going? How are they traveling?

> 📖 **Reading strategy**
>
> Check your understanding as you read.

AN EXTRAORDINARY EXPEDITION

DAY 1

I can't believe I'm finally in Antarctica! We had to wait for four days in Chile because the weather was too bad to fly. Our plane arrived last night and we camped in tents on the **ice**. I didn't sleep much because there isn't any darkness during the Antarctic summer. Now I can say that I saw the midnight sun!

When I got up this morning, I saw how beautiful this place is. Of course, it's **freezing** too. There's only snow and ice as far as you can see. Oh, and there are also lots of **penguins**! I feel excited and ready to start our expedition to the **South Pole**. It's time to put on our skis …

DAY 8

It's the end of the first week. Our progress is good. For almost ten hours a day, there's no sound but the wind and our skis. The landscape is amazing. There are gigantic icebergs which take our breath away. Pulling the heavy sleds is tough. We've got all our fuel and food for the **expedition** behind us. But as we ski on, the sleds get lighter. And every night we camp under the stars.

SLED

4 Number the sentences in order.

☐ They met a scientist.
☐ They camped under the stars.
☐ The weather got worse.
☐ They started skiing.
☐ Luis had an accident.
[1] They arrived in Antarctica.

168

DAY 40

The weather got worse today. The **temperature** fell to 20 **degrees** below zero and there's a lot more snow. The wind is stronger, so skiing is more difficult. The climate here is crazy!

By lunchtime, we were all exhausted, so we stopped to rest. Suddenly, we heard a scream. One of the skiers, Luis, fell into a **deep crack** in the ice and hurt his leg. There isn't any medical help here, so we put him on a sled. Now we have to take turns to pull him. Things just got harder.

DAY 55

Success! We're at the South Pole at last! We set up camp near the research station yesterday evening, and Luis saw a doctor. Today we visited the research station and found out about the work they do here. One of the scientists showed us some ice cores. Scientists study ice cores to find out about the Earth's climate.

Luis is OK and we can all travel back to Chile by plane tomorrow. It's the end of an incredible experience and I'm sad to leave this beautiful place.

RESEARCH STATION

ICE CORE

5 Discuss with a friend.

1. Would you like to go to Antarctica? Why? / Why not?
2. Why do people go on expeditions?
3. Would you like to take part in an expedition in another country? Where?

Grammar 1

1   Watch Part 1 of the story video. Where are they? Who lives there? Then read and complete.

There _____ ice everywhere.
There _____ whales in the ocean, and
there _____ a lot of penguins and dolphins.

2 Read the grammar box and circle.

Grammar

Things we can count with numbers: There can be one or more than one of them.

There are a lot of **skiers**. **There aren't** any **scientists**. **Are there** any **penguins** in Antarctica? Yes, **there are**.

Things we can't count with numbers: There can't be more than one of them.
milk (a bottle of milk)   **snow** (three buckets of snow)
land (a piece of land)   **chocolate** (two bars of chocolate)

There's a lot of **snow**. **There isn't** any **oil**. **Is there** any **sunlight**? No, **there isn't**.

We use *there is* (or *there's*) for things we **can** / **can't** count.
We use *there are* for more than one thing we **can** / **can't** count.

3 Read *An Extraordinary Expedition* again and circle *there's/there isn't* and *there are/there aren't*.

170

4 Can you count these? Look and check (✓) or cross (✗).

1 ☐ sugar   2 ☐ shark   3 ☐ mountain   4 ☐ traffic

5 Look at the pictures in Activity 4 and say.

> There's sugar on the table.   There are sharks in the water.

Listening and Speaking 1

 Speaking strategy

Check the listener has understood.

6 Listen and write the answers.
2-32

1 What's the population of Japan? ....
2 What's the climate like? ....
3 What's the temperature in Tokyo in the summer? ....
4 What's the temperature in Tokyo in winter? ....
5 What animals live there? ....

7 Ask and answer about the Arctic. Use the questions in Activity 6 to help you.

The Arctic
Population: 4 million
Climate: winter – freezing, summer – cold, spring and fall – very short
Temperature at the North Pole: -40 to 0 degrees
Animals: Arctic wolf, Arctic fox, polar bear

171

Vocabulary 2

1 Listen and repeat.
2-33

fur · octopus · hunt · krill · feather
layer · migrate · poisonous · wing · waterproof

2 Listen and number.
2-34

3 Think and write a word from Activity 1 for each group.

1 a .... plant/spider/snake
2 soft/thick/real ....
3 a .... watch/coat/camera
4 a .... of bricks/clothes/paint

4 Read and solve the riddles with a friend.

1
I live in the ocean.
I'm not a mammal.
I'm good at hiding.
I have eight legs.
I'm an ....

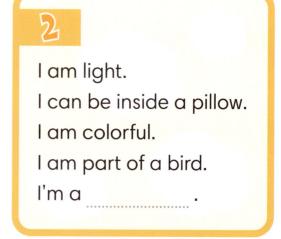

2
I am light.
I can be inside a pillow.
I am colorful.
I am part of a bird.
I'm a ....

Pre-reading 2

1 **Read the article and complete the chart.**

Reading strategy

Use charts to help you organize information.

How the whistling rat adapts to its habitat

Body	Food	Behavior
	plants close to home	

ADAPTING to the Kalahari

Whistling rats live in the Kalahari Desert in southern Africa. The Kalahari is a very dry habitat. There's no rain in winter for six to eight months. It's hot during the day, but temperatures can fall to −12 degrees Celsius at night. The ground is sandy, and there aren't many plants or trees.

Whistling rats have sandy-colored fur and this helps them hide in the desert. They have short, round ears, and they can hear very well. They give a loud whistle when a snake or a bird comes close. Then they run very quickly and jump into their holes underground. They're usually herbivores, and they eat plants not far from home, so they can escape easily when danger is close.

2 **Read the article again and answer.**

1. Why does the whistling rat have sandy-colored fur?
2. Which animals hunt the whistling rat?
3. Why does the whistling rat live underground?

173

Reading 2

3 Read *Adapting to Antarctica*. How do you think animals adapt to living in Antarctica?

> **Reading strategy**
> Use charts to help you organize information.

Adapting to Antarctica

Antarctica has the most extreme climate on Earth. For six months of the year, it's winter, and it's dark all day and all night. Then for six months, it's summer, and there are 24 hours of sunlight. Antarctica is also one of the windiest, driest places on Earth. Even in the summer the temperature never rises above freezing. So it's not surprising that you don't see many animals on the ice. However, the oceans around Antarctica are full of life. How do the animals survive? Let's meet some of the amazing inhabitants of Antarctica.

Leopard seal

Leopard seals hunt in the freezing, blue water around Antarctica. They're very successful predators. They use their long, sharp teeth to catch penguins and fish. Leopard seals have dark gray **fur**, and this helps to camouflage them while they **hunt**. The fur also keeps the seals warm on land. In the water, a thick **layer** of fat below their skin does the same job. The fat also helps them through the long, hard Antarctic winters. Leopard seals can survive for two months without eating.

Leopard seal

Antarctic octopus — tentacle

Antarctic octopus

The purple Antarctic **octopus** is big and **poisonous**. It has a special chemical in its blood that stops it from freezing. Scientists put the same chemical in frogs, and the frogs survived the cold, too. The Antarctic octopus eats snails and fish that it catches with its long tentacles. It uses poison to kill its food, like a snake.

Adélie penguin

Adélie penguins are small, noisy birds that live in Antarctica in the summer months. In winter, they **migrate** to warmer oceans. Like all penguins, they cannot fly, but they are excellent swimmers. They don't have **wings**, they have strong, flat flippers. They need to swim fast to catch fish and **krill**. The Adélie penguin has a layer of fat under its skin that keeps it warm, and **waterproof feathers** to help it stay dry. There are no trees, branches, or leaves in Antarctica, so Adélie penguins use rocks to protect their eggs and chicks.

4 Read the article again and complete the chart.

How Antarctic animals adapt to their habitat

	Body	Food	Behavior
Leopard seal			
Antarctic octopus			
Adélie penguin			

5 Answer the questions with a friend.

1. How long does winter last in Antarctica?
2. Why do leopard seals have dark gray fur?
3. How does the Antarctic octopus survive the cold in Antarctica?
4. What helps the Adélie penguins stay dry?
5. Why do Adélie penguins make nests with rocks?

Grammar 2

1 ▶ 11-3 BBC Watch Parts 2 and 3 of the story video. What's on the ice? Where do they find a clue? Then read and complete.

2 Read the grammar box and complete the rule.

> ### Grammar
>
> Describing words in a sentence go in a fixed order. The order depends on what each word is describing and it is: size, shape, colour, place/origin.
>
> > big   A   round   Antarctic Octopus   purple
>
> _____
> _____

Look at that _____, _____ octopus. What's it doing here?

3 Look, read and complete.

> black and white   blue   silver and red
> Amazon   large   long   ~~small~~   pink

1. They are *small,* _____ fish.

3. It's a _____ _____ killer whale.

2. It's a _____ _____ dolphin.

4. They are _____ _____ fish.

4 Readt *Adapting to Antarctica* again and circle the descriptions that have more than one describing word.

5 Choose describing words and a name to make phrases. You don't have to use a describing word from every column.

Size	Color	Origin	Name
big	white	African	monkey
small	brown	Arctic	hare
enormous	gray and white	Japanese	wolf
tiny			leopard

1 .... 3 ....
2 .... 4 ....

Listening and Speaking 2

6 Listen and use the questions to write notes about one of the animals.

Southern Right whale

Emperor penguin

Sooty albatross

1 What's its name?
2 Where does it live?
3 What is it?
4 How many are there in the world today?
5 Why is it in danger?
6 What can we do to save it?

7 Work with a friend who wrote notes about a different animal. Ask and answer the questions in Activity 6.

177

Writing

1 Read Amanda's report.
Why are blue whales in danger?

2 Read Amanda's report again.
Find words that mean …

1 very small ....
2 very big ....
3 very interesting ....

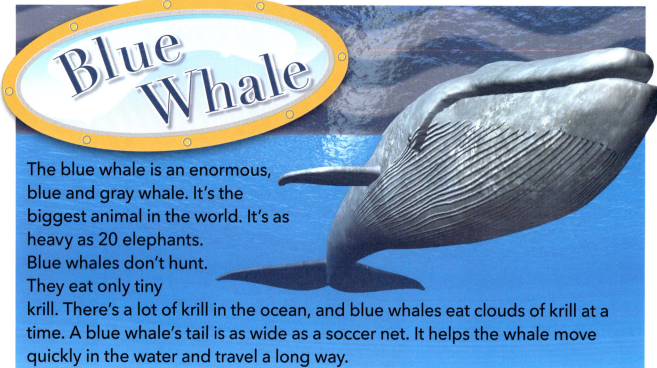

Blue Whale

The blue whale is an enormous, blue and gray whale. It's the biggest animal in the world. It's as heavy as 20 elephants.
Blue whales don't hunt. They eat only tiny krill. There's a lot of krill in the ocean, and blue whales eat clouds of krill at a time. A blue whale's tail is as wide as a soccer net. It helps the whale move quickly in the water and travel a long way.

Sadly, blue whales are in danger because hunters killed them until 1966. People ate whale meat, burned whale oil as fuel, and used whalebones to make clothes and umbrellas. Now people cannot hunt blue whales. I hope we can save this fascinating animal.

3 Read the report again. Find and circle the extreme descriptions in the report.

4 Find or draw pictures of an animal in danger. Then go to the Workbook to do the writing activity.

Writing strategy

Use extreme descriptions to make your writing stronger. *The blue whale is an enormous, blue and gray whale. It's the biggest animal in the world. A blue whale's tail is as wide as a soccer net.*

Now I Know

1 Why is Antarctica special? Look back through Unit 11 and complete the sentence in different ways.

> Antarctica is special because …
> it's the coldest place on Earth.

2 Choose a project.

Interview a scientist who works in Antarctica.

1 Work in pairs. Think of the scientists in Antarctica. What do they study? What's their life like?
2 Write an interview with a scientist and practice it.
3 Perform it to the class.

or

Research an extreme habitat.

1 Think of an extreme habitat and do some research.
2 Make a poster with pictures and key words about the habitat.
3 Write about where it is, what it's like, animals that live there, and how they adapt.
4 Show your poster to the class.

Read and circle for yourself.

I can identify key details in factual conversations.

I can understand the main points in descriptive texts about animals.

I can act out a short dialog with a friend.

I can write factual descriptions of animals.

12

Why do we have festivals?

Listening
- I can understand most details in conversations about festivals.

Reading
- I can understand the main points in descriptive texts about festivals.

Speaking
- I can describe a special event.

Writing
- I can use time phrases to write about a future event.

1 Look at the picture and discuss.

1 Who can you see at this special meal?
2 What time of year do you think it is?
3 What decorations are there? How do they show the season?
4 Which important holidays do you celebrate with your family?

2 Discuss with a friend.

1 What's your favorite festival?
2 When is it? What do you celebrate on that day?
3 Do you wear special clothes?
4 What do you do?
5 What festivals from other countries do you know?

3 Watch the video. Read and circle.

1 This is a **Chinese** / **Japanese** festival.
2 People **dance** / **sing** in the street.

181

Vocabulary 1

1 **Listen and repeat.**

lantern — parade — emperor — stilt walker — annoying

hang — crowded — 1 costume — furry — fireworks

2 **Listen and number.**
2-38

3 **Think and write a word from Activity 1.**

1 hairy   _furry_   3 put up ....
2 walking on sticks ....   4 lamp   ....

4 **Think and write a word from Activity 1 for each group.**

1
wear a
put on a ....
make a

2
       street
a .... room
       bus

3
watch a
take part in a ....
dance in a

4
a .... party

182

5 Discuss with a friend.

1 When did you last see fireworks?
2 When did you last watch a parade? Do you sometimes take part in a parade?
3 When did you last wear a costume? Who made it?
4 What do you find annoying?

Pre-reading 1

1 Read the beginning of a story. Then cover it and retell it in your own words to a friend.

> **Reading strategy**
>
> Retell a story in your own words.

THE SUITCASE

It was December 31st, and Ana and her family were almost ready to celebrate New Year.

"Go and put on your new dress," said Ana's mom. "It's eight thirty already!"

Ana ran up to her room to put on her best clothes. She was very excited. New Year was her favorite celebration. She loved the special meal that they ate only once a year, and the fireworks at midnight. This year, she was even more excited because her uncle, aunt, and cousins were on their way. They lived in the south of Argentina, and Ana didn't see them often.

The buzzer rang, and Ana got to the door first. There stood her uncle and his family. "Hi, Ana! It's so good to see you again," said Aunt Cristina. "I have something important for later!" Ana looked down at the suitcase in her aunt's hand. She wondered what was inside.

2 What traditions do your family have on New Year's Eve? Discuss with a friend.

Reading 1

3 🎧 2-39 Read *The Lantern Festival*. Where did they find Andrew's little brother?

Reading strategy
Retell a story in your own words.

The Lantern Festival

"Can I go to the **Lantern** Festival with Mai? Please, Mom?" asked Andrew. His mom smiled, "Yes, you can. But you have to take your little brother with you." "No! I won't go!" shouted Andrew's brother. "And I won't carry a lantern." "You're so **annoying**, Harry," said Andrew. "You will go with us, and that's final!"

rice balls

Later they met Andrew's friend Mai at the festival. There were people everywhere. The children watched the **stilt-walkers** in the **parade**, and Andrew tried rice balls for the first time. "This is my favorite Chinese festival," Mai said. "Tonight, it will be the first full moon of the year. It's the end of the Chinese New Year celebrations."

4 Read the story again. Answer the questions.

1. What did Andrew eat at the Lantern Festival?
2. When is the Lantern Festival?
3. Why did it get more difficult to find Harry?
4. Why did Andrew hold Harry's hand at the end?

5 Retell the story in your own words. Use words from the box.

| After that | Finally |
| First | Next | Then |

184

"There's a good story behind the Lantern Festival. Many years ago, the Jade **Emperor** was very angry with the people in a **village**. He said they killed his favorite goose. 'I will send firestorms, and I will destroy your village,' he threatened. A good-hearted fairy warned the villagers, and they **hung** red lanterns all over town. When the emperor saw the lanterns, he thought the village was on fire already. So, he didn't send a firestorm, and the village was safe."

"That's so interesting, Mai. Now I understand what all these red lanterns mean."

"Do you want to solve a riddle?" Mai asked. "You can win a prize. Here, look inside this lantern."
"I won't win. I never do!" said Andrew, laughing.

Suddenly, he looked around. "Harry! Where's Harry? He's lost!" Andrew shouted for his little brother. He was very worried. They looked everywhere, but they couldn't find Harry.

Just then, people in colorful lion **costumes** came past. "Oh, dear! The lion dance is starting. It's even more **crowded** than before," said Mai, "It will be more difficult to see Harry."
"Look!" said Andrew, pointing, "Those **furry** legs are shorter than the others." They looked closely and, sure enough, Harry was under a lion costume, happily moving with the dancers.

hold hands

After the lion dance, they stayed to watch some amazing **fireworks**. Andrew held his brother's hand tightly. "Let's keep together from now on," he said.

185

Grammar 1

1   Watch Parts 1 and 2 of the story video. Why doesn't the Smogator want Jack to end his quest? Then read and circle.

I want to / We'll find him after the dragon dance.

2 Look at the grammar box and read.

> ### Grammar
>
> **will and won't**
>
> You/He **will** find his family.   I/We **will not** be at school next week.
>
> We**'ll** see a lot of fireworks.   Alice/They **won't** finish early tonight.
>
> There**'ll** be rice balls.
>
> 1 To make a positive prediction about the future use ___will___ .
> 2 To make a negative prediction about the future use *will not* or _____ .
> 3 *Will* _____ change depending on the person.

3 Read *The Lantern Festival* again and circle sentences with *will* and *won't*.

186

4 Write the words in order.

1 seven/thirty/get/up/at/I'll

....

2 eight/I/o'clock/at/won't/get/up

....

3 see/We'll/a/mountains/lot of

....

4 Dad/early/tonight/get home/will

....

Listening and Speaking 1

> **Speaking strategy**
>
> Ask questions to get other people talking

5   **Look and match. Then listen and check.**

1 Thanksgiving   a December 31st
2 New Year's Eve   b July 4th
3 U.S. Independence Day c second Sunday in May
4 Valentine's Day   d February 14th
5 Mother's Day   e fourth Thursday in November

6 **Make predictions about Mother's Day for you and your family. Discuss with your friends.**

> Next Mother's Day I'll probably make my mom a gift. What about you?

American English

04/01   April first.

British English

01/04   April the first.
         The first of April.

> I think we'll visit my grandma.

187

Vocabulary 2

1 **Listen and repeat.**

2 **Listen and number.**

3 **Read and write a word from Activity 1.**

1 We're only playing. The water is spraying!
2 Move me around and I make a loud sound.
3 You can eat me. I grow on a tree.
4 It's time to rest. Today is the best!
5 Now I'm small. I'll be this when I'm tall.
6 I look like a snake, but I live in a lake.
7 I'm covered in glue and I don't know what to do.

4 **Discuss with a friend.**

1 Did anyone in your family get married recently?
2 Is there a special food you eat during a celebration?
3 When do your parents have a day off? What do they do?

Pre-reading 2

1 Read the article. Where will Noriko go and why? What will she take with her?

Reading strategy

Compare the information in a text with your own life and culture.

Hanami

We asked Noriko, from Japan, about a famous festival that will take place next month.

Noriko, what is Hanami?

It's an ancient festival that happens when the cherry blossoms (the flowers on cherry trees) open. It's usually in March or April. Hanami means *looking at flowers* in Japanese.

Where will you go to look at cherry blossoms?

I'll go to the park with my family. There are a lot of beautiful trees there. We'll sit under the cherry trees and have a picnic.

What will you eat at the picnic?

We always take lunchboxes full of delicious food. This year, I'll also take wagashi, which are Japanese sweets, and cherry blossom biscuits, my favourites!

2 Discuss with a friend.

1. Do you know any other festivals that celebrate nature? When do they take place?
2. Do you like picnics? What do you usually eat at a picnic?
3. What special food do you only eat once a year?
4. Which foods come from your culture? Do people eat them in other countries?

Reading 2

3 🎧 2-43 Read *Spring Festivals Round the World*. Which festival seems like the most fun?

> 📖 **Reading strategy**
>
> Compare the information in a text with your own life and culture.

SPRING FESTIVALS ROUND THE WORLD

We spoke to school children from two very different countries.
We asked: *What will you do to celebrate spring this year? Where will you go? What will you eat?* and *What does the festival mean to you?*

Cambridgeshire, UK

This spring we'll celebrate the Ely Eel Festival. It happens every year at the end of April for three days. It's a new festival but we love it. It celebrates the city of Ely. Some people say our city takes its name from the **eel** – a long, slippery fish.

> Eels are symbols of good luck so some people **get married** on that day.

• On the first day, we'll walk in the parade, which starts near the **cathedral**. After that, we'll watch the eel-throwing competition in the market square. They won't be real eels! People make them with socks and put rice inside. After the competition, there'll be music and dancing and the town criers will ring their **bells**.

town crier

4 Read the article again. Write *E* (Eel Festival), *S* (Songkran), or *B* (both festivals).

1 People get wet.
2 It isn't an ancient festival.
3 People celebrate in the street.
4 It takes place in only one city.
5 People eat special food.
6 People visit their families.
7 There are competitions.
8 It's also a New Year festival.

Chiang Mai, Thailand

In Thailand, spring is the hottest time of the year. We've got an ancient celebration called Songkran in April. People celebrate all over the country.

This year, like every year at Songkran, people will have **water fights** in the streets. Children **have got a day off** school, so I'll spend the day **spraying** water over all my friends in the neighbourhood.

Grown-ups do different things at Songkran. This year my mum will visit my granny. She'll wash her hands with special water and clean her house.

There are lots of delicious things to eat at Songkran. My favourite is **sticky** rice with mango. It's a dessert made with **coconut** milk.

Songkran means *change* and the festival also celebrates Thai New Year. We wash away the old year and get ready for the new.

5 Discuss with a friend.

1. Do you have any festivals to celebrate the seasons in your country?
2. Are there any special places people visit in your country during festivals?
3. Does anything you read remind you of your life?

Grammar 2

1   Watch Part 3 of the story video. How does the Doctor save Jack from the dragon? Then read and complete.

.... you do?

2 Read the grammar box and complete with **A** and **B**.

Grammar

Questions about the future

a) **Who will you** invite next week?   I'll invite my friends.
   What will she do this year?   She'll go to high school.
   Where will he go?   He'll go to the movies.
   When will they arrive?   They'll arrive tonight.
   How will you get there?   I'll get there by bus.

b) **Will there be** fireworks at the Snow Festival? **Yes, there will.** / **No, there won't**.

1 Questions in group .... need *yes* or *no* in the answer.
2 Questions in group .... need information in the answer.

3 Read *Spring Festivals Round the World* again. Circle the questions with *will*.

192

4 Match the questions to the answers.

1 What will you do for your birthday party next week?
2 What time will the party start?
3 How will you get there?
4 How many friends will you invite?

a I'll invite four friends.
b The party will start at 4 p.m.
c We'll get there by car.
d We'll go to the movies.

Listening and Speaking 2

5 Listen and write the questions in the chart. Add two more questions.

Questions	My friend's answers
When will you learn to drive?	

6 Ask and answer the questions in Activity 5 with a friend and write his/her answers.

Can I ask you some questions about your future?

Yes, sure.

193

Writing

1 Look at Lisa's homework. Guess the answers to the questions.

1. Where and when are the Highland Games?
2. When and how did the Highland Games begin?
3. What will Lisa's dad do at the festival?
4. What will Lisa do?
5. What will Lisa wear?
6. Where will Lisa's mom be?
7. What are bagpipes?

2 Read Lisa's homework. Check your answers to Activity 1.

A festival I love: The Highland Games

Next weekend, it will be the Highland Games in my village. It's an ancient Scottish festival, and we celebrate it in the summer.

People think that the Highland Games started a thousand years ago. A king wanted to find the fastest runner in the land, so there was a race up a big hill. There are a lot of sports at the festival now, but there's also music and dancing.

This year, all of my family will go to the Games. My dad will be in the shot put competition. He has to throw a heavy stone. I'll do traditional highland dancing. I practice with my group twice a week. We wear special skirts called kilts and soft black shoes. My grandpa will watch me.

Next week, my mom will play the bagpipes in a different parade. Bagpipes are a musical instrument from Scotland. They are very loud, but I love them!

3 Read Lisa's homework again. Find and circle the time phrases.

4 **WB 169** Find or draw pictures of your favorite festival. Then go to the Workbook to do the writing activity.

Writing strategy

Use time phrases, e.g. *next weekend*, *in the summer*, *this year*, *next week* to write about the future. They help to structure your writing.

Now I Know

1   Why do we have festivals? Look back through Unit 12 and write more answers.

We have festivals to mark seasons.

2 Choose a project.

Find out about a festival costume.

1 Research traditional costumes people wear at festivals and choose one you like.
2 Find or draw pictures of the costume and label the different items of clothing.
3 Write about the costume and the festival.
4 Give your presentation to the class.

or

Invent your own festival.

1 Imagine a festival you would like to celebrate.
2 Decide what the festival celebrates.
3 Find or draw pictures and write information about it.
4 Make a poster about your festival.
5 Show your poster to the class.

Read and circle for yourself.

I can understand most details in conversations about festivals

I can understand the main points in descriptive texts about festivals.

I can describe a special event.

I can use time phrases to write about a future event.

Wordlist

Unit 1

Key vocabulary

above
along
around
art gallery
below
beside
bridge
building
close to
cross
down
downtown
harbor
map
museum
recreation center
sign
square
theater
up

Readings

aquarium
concert
dugong
giraffe
lucky
mistakes
ship
Sydney Opera House

Unit 2

Key vocabulary

archeologist
bury
careful
carnivore
dead
dig
dinosaur

exhibit
extinct
gold
herbivore
horn
loud
pharaoh
quick
steps
tail
thieves
tomb
treasure

Readings

bones
curator
discover
fossil
hieroglyphs
museum
paleontologists
temple
T-rex
Tutankhamun's mask

Unit 3

Key vocabulary

beautiful
blanket
camping stove
campsite
clean up
coast
compass
flashlight
get lost
go kayaking
go rock climbing
go zip lining
heavy
light
make a fire

meet new people
set up a tent
sleeping bag
unsafe
waterfall

Readings

certificate
course
cover
ground
hiker
hole
life vest
path
scary
scenery
trash can
tutor

Unit 4

Key vocabulary

bowl
castle
coin
enormous
fairy tale
fierce
furious
giant
hero
hide
husband
king
legend
myth
prince
princess
queen
search
silver
wife

Readings

ancient
ancient times

champion
civilisation
culture
cut down
god
fact
famous
focus
human qualities
knight
natural events
plot
rise
run after
sheriff
sunflower
take a deep breath
top
tradition
trap
trouble
wheat
woods

Unit 5

Key vocabulary

breathe
burn
coal
country
electricity
fossil fuel
fresh air
full
gadgets
habitat
insect
lungs
oil
plant
power plant
pretty
protect
rescue
throw away
wildlife

Readings

air pollution
bottle
butterfly
cycle
fumes
meadow
park ranger
plant a tree
rescue
rescue action
survive
switch off

Unit 6

Key vocabulary

century
cheap
choose
colorful
decade
expensive
gift
go shopping
half
hour
invent
minute
money
pay
quarter
second
shadow
stall
tell the time
useful

Readings

battery
boring
clock face
digital clock
earrings
hands
obelisk

pendulum
price
soap
spin around
stallholder
stationary stall
sundial
water level

Unit 7

Key vocabulary

afraid
band
cello
chess
clarinet
dream
drum
exciting
famous
hang out
headphones
magazine
modern
musician
orchestra
saxophone
string
traditional
trombone
trumpet

Readings

actor
audience
brass
comic
conductor
percussion
prize
queue
result
skills
strings
woodwind

Unit 8
Key vocabulary

bright
bump
cry
float
frightened
in a hurry
laboratory
launch
Moon
orbit
owl
planet
rocket
rude
scientist
space station
spacesuit
stick
telescope
worried

Readings

flight
horrible
once
repairs
robotic arm
rub
running machine
shine
sky
space walk
spacecraft
stationary bike
train (v)
voice

Unit 9
Key vocabulary

attic
balcony
basement
bricks
build
concrete
elevator
flat
metal
move
narrow
plastic
roof
stairs
steep
stone
sweep
view
wide
wood

Readings

canal
fall off
houseboat
land
neighbour (UK)
neighbourhood (UK)
ruin
skyscraper
swan

Unit 10
Key vocabulary

back
bandage
brain
cold
cough
fever
heart
muscles
neck
pale
rest
save your life
shoulder
sick
skin

sneeze
spread
stomach
take medicine
vaccination

Readings

alive
ambulance
audience
blood
broken leg
cover
crutch
disease
germs
handkerchief
hospital
kill
kingfisher
reason

Unit 11

Key vocabulary

continent
crack
deep
degrees
expedition
feather
freezing
fur
hunt
ice
krill
layer
migrate
octopus
penguin
poisonous
South Pole
temperature
waterproof
wing

Readings

Adélie penguin
Antarctic octopus
flipper
ice core
leopard seal
research station
sled
tentacle

Unit 12

Key vocabulary

annoying
bell
cathedral
coconut
costume
crowded
eel
emperor
fireworks
furry
get married
grown-up
hang
have a day off
lantern
parade
spray
sticky
stilt walker
water fight

Readings

Jade Emperor
rice balls
sticky rice
stilts
town crier